FROM FEAR TO FLOW HANDBOOK

HOW TO FLOURISH IN THESE UNPREDICTABLE TIMES

LIZ NOTTAGE

BY YOU, FOR YOU

From Fear to Flow Handbook

How to flourish in these unpredictable times

ISBN 978-1-5272-7051-0
Publisher: Elizabeth Alexis Nottage
Permission to use quotes from other authors
Wayne Dyer
Shakespeare
Rumi
Abraham Hicks
Anodea Judith
Credits for illustrations: pintrest.com
Credits for cover images: Lisa Armstrong
Contact : Liz Nottage
FB : Align Up Mindfully

Dedication

To all of you taking this courageous step on your path to self-discovery. Your bravery, dedication and commitment to becoming the fullest version of you in this moment of Now, is appreciated beyond words. You are changing the world and bringing us back to Oneness from your vulnerable heart and the invincible love radiating from it. You are loved in return, beyond measure.

Acknowledgements

To every single person I have ever had an encounter with, however transient or enduring, I remember you, and for me, every single second was wonderful and profound. I recognise the utter beauty you brought into my life. Those incredible Now moments that I will never forget. I understand that they brought me here, to this book and this Now moment. I think of you and those times with much love and eternal appreciation for the rainbow of distinct light you gave me, with which I could colour my life. This book is created by your love and your lessons and the unique and simple tapestry that we wove together. You live in my heart and I hope you can feel the love I send to you, in yours. My gratitude runs deep, and it makes me smile and cry, happy, as I feel the beautiful ache of remembrance. Thank you.

Table of Contents

Introduction

At this time of pandemic. As the world faces a crisis that we have not witnessed before in our lifetimes. As globally we face uncertainty and lots of confusion thanks to our blessed leaders. As many succumb to panic, fear and anxiety, it is a good idea to remember that the world was not normal before. Through this agent of change we are transitioning into a new and evolved way to exist and engage with ourselves, each other and our planet.

This handbook is a guide to assist you as you start moving from the fear, caused by these unpredictable times, into the flow of embracing our transformation and your part in it.
Flow comes from unity in our global collective and in yourself, as you align the holy trinity of your Superconscious, Conscious and Subconscious.
This book will take you on a journey of discovery and point you in the direction of where to find the research and support information you will need in your toolbox as you expand your awareness.
It is time to jump off the Corona-coaster Ghost Train and ease into the Tunnel of Love.
This book will help you to find and flow to your truth and

your freedom. These will become the fundamental tenets of our collective future.

Once you have read this and absorbed just how magnificent you are and how epic this adventure is, you can check out the mind-bending information that is at your fingertips.

Listed at the back are recommended books, YouTube channels, websites, healing modalities and practitioners that will make it easy for you to apply discernment to your own understanding of what is happening Now.

Chapter 1

Why you are here

Welcome dear one. You, reading this book and the truth within is no accident or coincidence. You scripted it before you came into physical. You are either now vibrating in total accordance with its frequency or planting the seeds for acceptance and application for when you are resonant. You are profoundly loved, as you bravely follow your heart, as it leads you through your questions to the answers within.

It will take strength and courage to start this journey, and it is not for the fainthearted. But that is why you are here. You are part of the vanguard blazing the trail home. You have a critical part to play as we move out of the shallows and into the deep mystic river of life. You are not alone, and you never have been, we go as one.

The reason you have come to this information is because of an unsettling feeling that there is more going on here than you have been told or led to believe. You have a curiosity, and a deep insistence that you want to break away from the belief systems and programmes you have been given, by parents, society, institutions, organized religions and governments etc. and find your own.

There are those you will encounter that have no concept of the truths held within this book, and no desire to seek them. That is fine, all is well, they are still the light of creation on their own path. There are many different ascension routes to the mountaintop.

You are reading this because you have been brought here by the more conscious part of you to receive the answers you are ready for.
THE most important thing to remember is that this is your journey and it is as unique to you as your fingerprint.
There are a lot of people wanting to assist you through this process, and that is all they want to do. There are many sources of information and many different modalities that will help you find the resonance, that you have realized, you need to find. This book will provide you with some guidance and information as you start on your quest for self-mastery, moving from fear to flow.

No one can walk this path for you, but as we are choosing this path together, we may accompany each other. There is so much support out there, for energetic hand holding, information sharing and light bearing through the darkness. We are a soul family and we uplift, empower and encourage each other along the way.
Only you will know what is 'right' for you, you will feel it resonate with you on a vibrational level. Use your own discernment as this book will give you lots of ideas and

leads for you to do your own research which is vital for a true path that is yours.

It has been difficult for some to take this path as they are so entrenched in the delivered doctrine, and what you are reading has been called woo woo, new age and hippie. To be honest there is only one answer to that, follow your own heart, do you own research, apply critical thinking, make up your own dear sweet individual mind.

As Dr. Wayne Dyer said "The ultimate ignorance is to reject something you know nothing about yet refuse to investigate"

Remember everyone is on their own mission, all set their own intention before coming here for this specific time. You are not accountable to anyone but you. Respect and cherish all your choices, as much as another's.

It starts by having those moments when you stop and question what is really going on. In your heart you feel a discord that you cannot explain, but it is causing you to want to search for answers that start making sense to you. It is a brave step in the direction away from everything you have been taught. The systems you have been made to adhere and subscribe to. The labels and identities with which you have been told to define yourself. The boxes you have been told to place yourself in, and if you could not do it, someone or some bigger entity would do it for you.

As long as you believed you were defined by what you had, what you did, what others thought of you, and, most destructive of all, that you are separate from everything else and the God that lives inside you. Then you are accepted.

You have been asked for millennia to give your power away. To live constantly in the twisted story of the past, whether your own or your countries, your race, your gender etc. You have been cowed by the stresses the future holds of lack, limitation and conflict.

Now, you are beginning to understand that none of this makes sense and you are reaching out with your heart to find your way, to your own truth. To the recognition that you are a divine being, and you hold the power of your own existence.

You have been living through the fear-based survival instincts of your ego self. This assisted you in the beginning, to keep you safe within a tribe that was as disconnected and grappling for sustenance as you. But now you understand that it is no longer necessary. You can let go of what no longer serves you as you move to embracing the true sovereignty of who you really are and start existing in alignment with your true nature. You are pure positive energy with a desire to express yourself. You are love made manifest.

Chapter 2

Who you really are

Do you remember when you were just vibration, a part of the first thought?
The first desire of creation to know itself that reverberated through the void, and thus our quantum universe of consciousness was created.
You are subatomic waves of energy.
You are the Universe exploring itself.

You are an eternal, limitless, multidimensional being having a temporary human experience, in a three-dimensional construct of reality, created with duality embedded into it so you can experience yourself. For how can you know light until you have experienced dark.
It is also so you can evolve, innovate and push the boundaries at the leading edge of expansion.
You are the Creator's desire to express itself. You are, quite literally, divine expression.

The Universe is All That Is, nothing can exist that is not part of the One. Quantum physics has shown that everything is entangled energy, a unified, connected field.

It is one infinite being of which you are a fractal. It is conscious and aware: Look around you, are you not amazed at the intricacies of what you see before you? The beauty, and the balance. The Universe is intelligence beyond anything you could ever hope to conceive of in your humanness. That is how it is supposed to be. For if you are All That Is, and you know you are everything, how do you experience what you are?

That, was the first thought, that was the first vibration, the first energy in motion. Creation began with a desire to experience itself. The intention to create, to express. The creation is creating itself still, this is evolution, this is who you really are. How beautiful and perfect is that. How incredible do you feel knowing that?

You are Divine Intention.

You are The All. The creator and the created in the process of unlimited creating.

You are a divine spark of The Universe, Source Energy, All That Is, The Unified Field, Conscious Awareness, God of so many names. The name doesn't matter, only the unchangeable truth matters.

In the book, to cancel the idea of separation, it will be called You, as often as possible.

When You are all that can exist, You exist in a state of unconditional divine love, contentment, maybe even smugness, as nothing can exist which is not You. It can be

no other way.
You, in your humanness, have beliefs that say you are
undeserving and need to prove worthiness. This is a
control mechanism and when intelligent thought is applied
you can see that it is unnecessary and impossible to prove
worthiness to yourself when you are All There Is.
Imagine you needed your little toe to prove its value or
you would condemn it.

The Universe (You) is all knowing. You in human form, are
providing the joy of unknowing. Knowing something
theoretically is not the same as experiencing it. That is why
you are here, and duality exists. To experience and
understand what 'thriving' is, those that thrive need to
have been those that suffer. Those that are 'good' need to
have been those that are 'bad' so that 'good' can be
experienced and understood beyond the theoretical. You
can know that you are all that is, but what does that mean,
it needs to be experienced. Being short is conceptual until
you stand next to someone who is tall, only then is it
known. You must love the differences unconditionally, as
they are all part of the whole.

You are energy vibrating at different frequencies. The
Universe is pure energy. That is what you and All That Is,
is. You can see it when you look at the sky, after
meditation it can look like code. It is the nature of things
and it is conscious.
It is aware. It is infinite. It is love and you are made of it,

surrounded by it, encased in it. You are existing, walking and living in floating love. It is Life, Prana, Chi, The Force. It is the air you breathe, the space between, the blade of grass, the ocean, the grain of sand. It is timeless, unlimited, continuous creation.

This conscious energy vibrates at differing frequencies. Matter is simply stored energy vibrating very slowly. You can control and manipulate this energy with the power of thought. The double slit experiment showed that all energy is in a wave form, until it is measured or observed. Quantum theory states that the whole is a sum of its parts, and that the whole is represented in each of its parts. This is essentially true when you look at fractals and patterns, from leaves to snowflakes. The Universe is replicating its larger self. You are a replica of your larger essence. The golden ratio is repeated in an eye to a galaxy. You are a fractal of Source energy, made in its image, meaning you have the same creative power. You are God.

There is no past or future these are illusionary constructs, manifested to allow the complex but limited human mind to experience cause and effect and duality.

The delayed choice quantum eraser experiments have shown that there is no time. The future changes the present, or expressed differently, the present changes the past. Quantum entanglement means every potential reality already exists in this Now moment.

There is no infinite time, there is only infinite possibility. There is only expansion Now. You are, in this moment, becoming more. You are the spiral of evolution.

When a fraction of you came from non-physical into
physical form, you agreed to forget who you really are.
This sensation of unknowing is supposed to be exhilarating
and provide the fertile environment from where great
expansion can occur.
You can reconnect at any time, so it is important that as
you continue reading, you understand the meaning of
alignment.
Alignment is when you are connected to the non-physical
part of you. It is when you are under the influence of your
higher self and where your true power lies.
Alignment is the seeking of your full potential in each Now
moment, fully cognizant of who you really are.
In this moment of Now there exists the pure potential
energy that only desires to express itself, that is you, that
is creation.

You chose to forget who you really are in this human
incarnation, because you knew it would lead to expansion.
You chose to forget so you could experience the utter joy
in remembrance. As you start on this journey you will
amplify your connection to the light you left on to show
you the way home. Your heart holds the truth of who you
are. Follow it, surrender to its wisdom. It will lead you
along the path of breadcrumbs you left for yourself, and
you will find your way back to your divine essence. This
epic adventure will be delightful, magnificent and enhance

the evolutionary process for The All.

This physical realm you have created, is such an incredible plane in which to know yourself through your five senses. You can create whatever you want and then experience what it looks like. How it feels to touch it, how it feels to have it touch you. You can listen to it and you can speak it or sing it. You can smell it and taste it. A full sensory experience of your artistry.

There is no end to what you can create and there is no death, you can do whatever you like, you have complete freedom, the divine gift of free will. You are so free you can choose to experience heaven on earth or hell on earth as this is the only place either can exist in this dimension of duality.
You are a wave of subatomic consciousness and just with your focused observation and elevated emotion you can collapse that wave into any particle reality you desire to experience in your delightful human form.

There are fundamental laws involved in the process of creation. The Law of Attraction is the one through which you are creating your reality.
You also have an innate guidance system installed.
Negative emotion is an indication that all is not well. It is a signal that changes need to be made. It is like a compass requiring a redirection back to satisfying emotions. Your

guidance system is never wrong. You will continue to feel negative emotion if you do not make the necessary adjustments. If you still do not make the necessary changes, your negative emotion will start to manifest as a physical ailment or psychological disorder. Or as extremely difficult external conditions. This is your guidance system trying to get your attention.

You made a promise to yourself through the Law of Attraction, that whatever you ask for it would be immediately given.

However, this ask and receive process is not done through words, but through vibration.

The Universe speaks in light frequency, vibration and sacred geometry. You are asking all the time through your vibrations and your emotions, which are energy in motion.

The Law Of Attraction states "That which is likened to itself is drawn" or "As you sow, so shall you reap"

To understand how you are creating your reality, you need to assimilate the fact that NOTHING is happening TO you. There is NO assertion or insertion. Everything that has ever happened or is happening is because vibrationally, you asked for it. Taking responsibility for this is tough for some, as it is much easier to believe that someone or something else is to blame and doing it to you. Well, there is NO ONE else. There is only YOU. And once you take this and own it as the powerful gift that it is, you can start deliberately creating your reality and the wondrous magic you wish to experience in this physical realm.

All emotions have their own frequency as shown in the diagram below. Those on the negative end of the scale, vibrate at a dense and lower frequency. Anger, guilt, resentment, irritation, frustration etc. When you are vibrating at this frequency, you will get more showing up in your reality that vibrates similarly. Ever noticed that when you are in a bad mood, things keep going wrong, spilled coffee, flat tyres, forgotten phones.
When you are in a good mood, feeling emotions on the upper, lighter end of the scale like appreciation, kindness, gratitude, happiness etc. Everything is always working out for you. Parking spaces right where you want them, friendly cashiers, green traffic lights.
YOU are, moment to moment, creating your experience through your vibration, so pay attention to how you feel. Your emotions are the inbuilt guidance system to call you back to alignment.

OMEGA

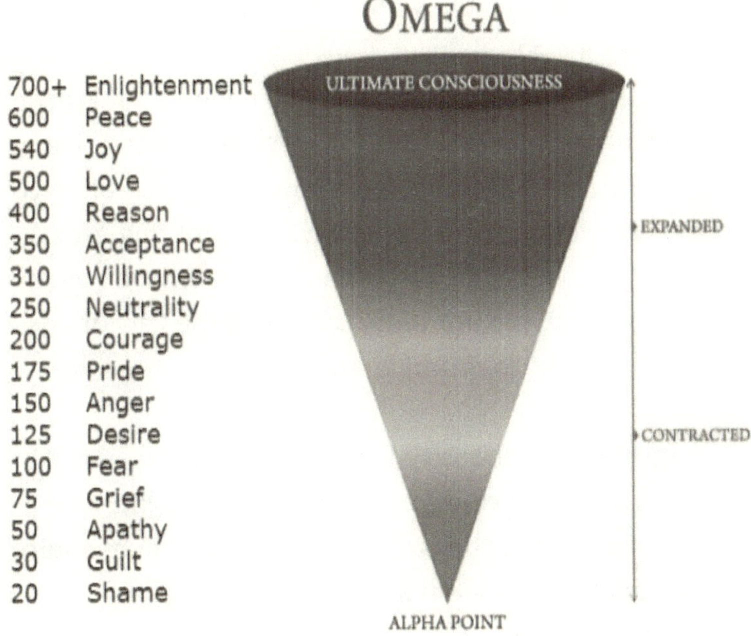

This is how it is designed to work.

You experience something you don't like. You feel a negative emotion that lets you know you want something that feels better. This causes you to ask for something you do like. The instant you ask, it exists, vibrationally. You then let go of the negative emotion, as it has served its purpose, and move into a positive emotional vibration. This means you are broadcasting the same frequency of what you do want, and it will be manifested into your physical reality. It will come as soon as you can consistently match the vibration of feeling it, believing it, having it, being it, doing it. It arrives effortlessly, as your thoughts and emotions line up. You could call this divine timing, but it is all You. This is the incredible creative power you have access to. It is how you are creating your observable reality. You are always transmitting a frequency of vibration. Mindfulness will ensure you are aware of what you are broadcasting to the Law of Attraction for it to return to you.

The most comprehensive teachings on this Universal Law of Attraction are from Abraham Hicks through Esther Hicks. Listening to the warmth and humour in her voice as she imparts the wisdom and knowledge of Abraham will instantly raise your vibration. They hold seminars, which you can access on YouTube, and have written many books on the Law of Attraction which I will list at the back of this book. These include processes to get it to work for you.

You are not meant to suffer. But if you keep feeling negative emotions and thinking negative thoughts. You will be choosing to feel bad most of the time. This will keep you discordant to the frequencies of what you want. And defies logic.
You are supposed to feel good, you are supposed to choose the good feeling thought and emotion, because why wouldn't you? Why have so many accepted, as their dominant vibration, the unhappy feeling of negative emotion? It is only there for you to use, to refine

your desires and to tell you when you are out of
alignment.

Most ask for their desires of more money, more food,
more friends, better sex from lower frequency emotions of
lack, desperation or fear. And though they are given
instantly vibrationally, unless you can raise your vibration
to match the higher frequencies of abundance, joy and
love, they will exist in a different dimension to you. You
must become a vibrational match to what you desire and
then you will attract it all into your physical reality.

And **attract** is the definitive word, it comes to you,
attracted by you.

You don't get what you want by 'doing'. Forced action
creates resistance.

You get what you want by 'being'. Inspired action from a
state of alignment, creates flow.

You can't find what you are missing, as the very act of
looking for it means it isn't there, and you are coming from
a place of loss.

Begging and desperation don't work either. You are
basically saying to the Law of Attraction I don't have it, it is
not in my experience and I want more of that please
(essentially you are creating more lack by emitting the
vibration of wanting).

The Law of Attraction is always fair. Everyone always gets
what they ask for. The laws of the Universe are not fickle.
This is why you are seeing two different realities existing
side by side. There are those in flow and those in fear.

You are awakening to this understanding and using this to

manifest magic in your life. You, reading this book, is a
manifestation you have created. As are repeating
numbers, synchronicities and the fortunate events that are
sometimes called 'lucky'.

The journey of self-discovery is your own, and it takes
courage and commitment, but the rewards are obvious,
the game of life becomes one of fun, connection and
purpose. You are recreating and redefining your world
through your expanding consciousness.
To be clear, so that there is no misunderstanding: You are
a creator being, it is the very fundamental nature of you,
to change, to deepen.
You, The Universe, not only wants to experience itself; it
wishes to know its capabilities. That is why the process of
evolution is never ending, there is always something new
to try. You thrive on change, it excites you, it pushes you
forward in divine cosmic momentum.
It thrills you and ultimately it is the defining Law of the
Universe, it is the **point of you..!!!**

If you try to resist, this, the very nature of you. You will
experience turmoil, despair, destruction and hardship as
you clamour to stay in a comfort zone that clearly is
holding you back from you own expansion. You must
understand that it is impossible, as futile as swimming
against a current. So, let it all go.
As you start vibrating at higher and higher frequencies and
start choosing experiences that resonate with yours, and

your environments highest good. You will find that lower frequency relationships, family members, pastimes, friends, locations, and jobs start to fall out of your reality. You may think this is sad, but it is not, this is the beauty of evolution. The experience has been lived and learned. It is time to move on to people and experiences that are more exhilarating and more in line with your new understanding of who you really are.

There will be new opportunities for divine expression, or shining your creator light. Feel no guilt: that is a distorted and dense control mechanism to stop you and hold you back from your expression. It serves neither you nor anyone else. It is just an excuse to not take responsibility for your expansion. An excuse to live someone else's idea for you. And allow you to resent them for it.

Do not stop yourself or anyone else from this incredible opportunity to take flight and soar ever higher in your understanding of self. That would be the GREATEST disservice you can perpetrate on yourself and any other.

Your reconnection to the infinite void, will fill the one within you, so you do not need drugs, you do not need drink, you do not need these addictions. There is no need for escapism when you can access the energy and power within you and your alignment. Choose to become addicted to elevated emotions and thoughtforms. Choose the open field of unlimited dreams not the pointlessness of incarceration in your own negative thoughts.

If you are unsure what alignment is and what it can look like, watch Lionel Messi play football. You are witnessing someone so in synch with the larger part of himself, playing with the passion of inspired action. He is art in motion, in complete connection to Source energy. Look at the expression on his face, the love made visible, it is divine flow personified.

You are only limited by the experience you are choosing to have. You can't run away from exposure to self lies and limitation. That was never going to be a part of the plan you created for your life, and that is why you are here reading this book.

There is a reason why people are angry and scared and manifesting the lives that they don't want. They are radiating the frequency of lack and undeserving. They feel they need to prove themselves worthy. The people around them cannot give them the acceptance they seek as they are on the same spinning wheel of vibratory reflection. This is a spiraling vicious circle of needing validation from each other that helps no one. Causing despair, recriminations and desperate destroyed expectations that cannot be fulfilled by people not coming from a place of wholeness.
The Universe already knows you are worthy and perfect, as you are a spark of it. You are it.

No succour is going to come to you from any external
source. It can only come from within. You must do the
inner work. Pull back from 'doing' and focus on 'being'.
Become attuned to how you feel and supremely conscious
of your vibration. Stop reacting. Stop being defensive.
Start taking active control over the only thing you have any
control over, which is your emotional state. When you give
that away to another, you are literally giving your power
away.
There are people that you will encounter that cannot
calibrate to their larger essence, and in their misalignment
they will manipulate. They are seeking a transient and
toxic high from any reaction whether positive or negative
that they can reap. You will notice that your emotions will
feel unsettled around this behaviour as you recognize the
dissonance. This is a person completely severed from their
connection. Do not pity them or react. In their
diminishment, they are teaching you wholeness. You have
become more from their lesson, from their gift. Be grateful
and understand your completion in that moment.
You have been installed with the software to help you, an
emotional vibratory feedback loop.
When you feel anger, it is mostly caused by powerlessness.
A feeling of being misunderstood or enslaved and
restricted. You can let that all go by accepting that no one
needs to understand you, you are love personified. No one
can control or enslave you when you understand you are
boundless.

Do not renounce your divine freedoms for comfort zones that reek of limitation and suffering.

Be tenacious in your revelation of self.

You can use the things that trigger you to help you uncover and change the patterns and beliefs that are affecting you and withholding from you all your power. These moments are of extreme value. Providing the opportunity for more growth and expansion in your human quest towards divinity and balance.

Everything in front of you is a mirror that you are holding up to yourself, so you can see the debilitating patterns that you need to change. They will keep reappearing and repeating, until you address the lesson and rebalance yourself back into your power.
All lessons are about the disempowerment of yourself in not accepting that you are entirely responsible for the creation of your life. That you need nothing external for your evolution within. You put this safeguard here to ensure your path home to mastery was always lit.
To explain this. Perhaps you find it difficult to set clear boundaries. You get an unconscious need met when people think you are 'nice'. They then take advantage of you. The mirror is showing you that you have chosen external validation of others over your own empowerment

and becoming your own master.

Remember you cannot get it wrong, and you will never be finished, as you are creators, it is what you are. You are creation, creating.

There is nothing that you need to achieve, attain or accomplish. Stop the delusion that you are a disappointment, stop your self-criticism. All you need to 'be' is happy, you are the perfection you have created. Be kind to yourself, for only then can you be truly kind to another. Love yourself, for only then can you truly love another.

Have you noticed repeating destructive patterns in your life? The same codependent or abusive relationships, the same controlling bosses, or hardship faced. This is because your reality is simply a reflection of what you believe you deserve, a reflection of how you perceive yourself and a projection of your idea of worthiness.

What you are creating is revealing how you see yourself. You are a continuous energetic vibratory signature calling towards you that which you are emitting. If you expect the best because you know you are perfectly deserving, that is what you will receive. Understanding your inherent flawlessness will change your life experience. Your reality is a literal mirror of how you feel about yourself.

Choosing this path of self-discovery takes immense

courage, it is a quest for revealing your true self. First you must face yourself and let go of limiting beliefs as you move forward. To start making decisions based on love, not made in fear. This has been described as doing the inner work, the dark night of the soul. It is where you strip yourself bare and take a deep dive into the personality you have created for yourself but isn't really you. It is the segment of a story that you choose to tell and define yourself by. Often, it depends on what you think the listener wants to hear or what you think you need to tell them to get them to like, love, pity or respect you. This is distorted as it can never be the whole story as you leave out the most important part. The intrinsic cosmic truth of you.

You are not who you think you are.

Your personality is just a projection of all the traits that were rewarded when you were growing up, and the closeted shadow side of those that were criticized. These are based on the belief systems of your parents and your environment. Then there is your history, a choice of what you wish to remember and retell, dependent on your desire of how you want others to perceive you. How others perceive you, is then based on their own upbringing, belief systems and what emotion they need to feel from you.
Essentially, your personality, to you, is an illusion.
To others it is an assumption.

Therefore your personality as a definite construct, does not exist.

The only time you truly exist is in the moment of Now where you define yourself with your next choice, of word, thought and action. This is total freedom.

This is the most liberating information you will ever absorb. You are defined by nothing except this incredible Now moment.

For example, you meet a new person. They offer you a cigarette. In that moment you are both a smoker and a non-smoker (just like Schrodinger's Cat). If you choose not to take the cigarette, the person will assume you are a non-smoker. You are defined by yourself in that moment and an assumption is made, unless the person has understood the concept written above. If that is the case, they will have no assumption or judgement as they recognize the newness and opportunity presented in each Now moment. This freedom allows you to throw off the shackles of the past and to never be subjected to any limitations imposed by subjugation to beliefs. It allows you to be the authentic creator of whoever you choose to be, Now.

When someone asks you who you are and what is your story, tell them "Everything that I have experienced has brought me to you as I am right now, with the ability to choose in this next moment the highest choice for myself, and I stand before you in utter appreciation of that one truth."

Don't allow the tentacles of the past to drag you back to density, there is no therapy there.
All that you do is miss this moment of Now and it is only here that you are making the choices that will define and create your future.
The future is fluid, there is no predetermination, only unlimited potential. It is only possible to create wonder from the Now moment. Never from the distraction of the past.

Observational Gifts

Look around at the obvious devotion from you and by you. These are the breadcrumbs you put there so you would know you are not alone. As you journey back to the full comprehension of Oneness, you will see all the signs you are projecting into your reality from your awareness within. Repeating numbers, songs, synchronicities and manifestations. The Universe has always had your back, is at your back, and leaping in front of you. Showing divine love in the form of butterflies, birdsong, chocolate, clouds, sunsets, music, peanut butter, the smile from a stranger, the thump, thump of your dog's tail. Love is everywhere, begging you to notice. You keep looking for something wonderful to come to you.

It Has.
It is.
You are.

You have 0.07 volts per cell and trillions of cells, you are
literally giving off trillions of volts from your amazing body.
You are firing frequencies as you function, think, see and
move. You are fundamental energy with a signature so
strong it creates the world around you. The Universe is
responding continuously to your vibratory symphony.

You are the Universe and You are singing You.

Understand this is what you are made of. Everything is
You, nothing cannot be God, Source energy. Your thoughts
and emotions create thoughtform and vibration that
manifest. You get into vibratory alignment with this Source
energy. It is not something you do and then it's 'done' and
you can go back to your past/ future worries. It is a state of
'being' in synch always. Living in flow, living intuitively
guided.
It is continuous awareness.
Let go of everything that does not serve you. That does
not allow ease and flow through attunement with Source.
And, crucially, understand that you are only responsible
for your own alignment. You are not responsible for
anyone else's. Believing that you are, is disempowering,
arrogant and in most cases enabling a pattern of
behaviour that serves no one. It is a belief that has the

debilitating potential of holding both or more souls back from advancing and finding their own cohesion. Cultivate heart-based, divine selfishness. It is the greatest gift you can give yourself and another, allowing each to expand forward without the chains of external validation and misplaced, destructive, conditional love.

It is quite a jump to get from a place of unworthy and powerlessness, to you are a divine spark of creation, but that's the mind-bending journey of the remembering. Be aware that you can only interpret your life and your projected reality, based on your level of consciousness. This is a quest for self-mastery, for becoming more than you can imagine. You are at the crossroads of your destiny where you can choose the path of spirit and the Fifth Dimension (5D) or the path of illusion in the Third Dimension (3D).

This is your **choicepoint** right here, an opportunity to jump to your highest timeline.
Stay and witness the 3D world descend into chaos or ascend with Gaia (our New Earth's name) as she moves to 5D consciousness.

All you have to do is let go of your attachment to your identity, the labels of your personality, the conformity and limitation of your boxes, and accept your boundlessness. Accept and live the paradox of your oneness and your uniqueness, your exceptional expansive expression.

Chapter 3

What is happening now

On Earth now, we are in the throes of a mass ascension from a third density experience to a fifth density experience. These levels of density are indicative of how much light is contained within any dimension. Light holds information, the more light available, the more information you can access for limitless expression. The fifth dimension is not a place. It is state of 'being', a level of consciousness. It is the understanding and acceptance of the magnificence of you, and your ability to create more, with access to more light and inherent information.

Deep down we all realised that we could not keep going down the path of destruction which we had created. Damaging our planet and losing touch with ourselves and each other. Collectively our hearts were screaming 'STOP'!!! And so, we did... As a global consciousness we created Corona or Covid-19. These are interesting and exciting times, if you can see the opportunity we have given ourselves. If you wish to go back to how it was before, you are missing the point entirely.

You have learned in your physics lessons that energy cannot be destroyed it can only be transformed from one state to another. On your planet you are literally watching the cleaning and cleansing of all the negative energy that you have sustained by your focus upon it. As it becomes exposed to the light it is then transmuted, liberated back to neutrality. You are watching these old control systems crumble away, as you focus on a new and empowering future.

The world is split in two. Those that are caught up in the negativity and the injustice. Focused on the crumbling structures, with predominant emotions of fear, anger, victimhood and blame. The others that are calm, appreciative, compassionate, and you can clearly see how they are deliberately creating their lives with manifestations based on ease and flow. The others are creating by default from knee-jerk reactions. For one section of the population things are working out just fine and for the others there is struggle, difficulty and stress. Maybe now you are asking the question; "Which one is me?"

Perhaps better questions are;

"Now I can see through the eyes of Source, what do I see?"

"When the Divine is me, how will I live?"

So now, with the world at varying levels of lockdown, imagine the world you would want to live in.

Write it down and feel the emotion of living in this New Earth. Visualize it, your thoughts combined with the corresponding emotion have immense power. Imagine a healed Gaia, a world of unlimited abundance, green and blue and in balance and thriving.

Where everybody has access to food, shelter, clean water and energy.

Where we live in communities of heart-based sustainability. Where everyone has the chance to explore their creativity. You swim, play, grow your own food, climb trees, build beautiful crafts and release your art, in music, dance, storytelling and innovation.

Where you are so in tune with the higher aspect of your connection that you can heal yourself, communicate telepathically, speed grow your vegetables through your ability to direct energy flow.

Where you release your clueless, and fumbling governments and institutions from the responsibility of taking care of you. Where you take your power back.

You have an opportunity here, that has never happened before in human history.

Do not waste it by focusing only on perceiving the negative, and look at the positive outpouring of love that started from the balconies of Italy.

We have the power as a collective to recreate our world as we move from the darkness into the light.

You (The Universe) did not, not have a plan. This process has been happening for many years, the Mayans predicted it on their calendar, that we would move from the age of Pisces into the age of Aquarius in 2012. Anodea Judith has posited that humanity has been evolving through the chakra system as a global collective. Starting when we were living in our Root chakra, focused on survival and our primary needs of food and shelter, we then moved through the Sacral chakra of creation and reproduction. Now, right at this moment, we are transitioning from the Solar Plexus chakra of will and force and into The Heart chakra of compassion and kindness. As she says we are moving from the 'Love of Power' into the' Power of Love'. This is being assisted by massive amounts of energy coming into our bodies and our planet Gaia. We are being upgraded in our DNA and our sacred geometry. We are receiving downloads and lightcodes to realign our human bodies that have been subjected to density for eons. We are moving to the higher frequency dimensions and our bodies need time to adjust and assimilate to the faster vibration of energy. We are moving from a 3D consciousness to a 5D consciousness. We are beginning to understand that we are energetic beings as we move away from service to self to service to others. We are realizing that the things we did before are not working or resonating with us anymore. Many are crumbling away, as there is not enough energy of the mass consciousness to sustain them. We want to start coming from our hearts and finding fulfillment in our authenticity. We will change our world with choices made from integrity and honour, not manipulation and fear.

This is the time of the great Awakening, and we (because we are all extensions of Source energy) all planned this, we designed this.

When you came from non-physical to become physical on Earth. You agreed you would forget your limitless divinity. Your human vessel is the avatar you chose for this video game of life. You designed yourself and the game in its entirety. You did this so you could experience lack, scarcity and fear. Then you would experience the rediscovery of your true nature and power, and change your world and the game, to start living in abundance, love and limitless potential.

You have never been abandoned or alone in this endeavour. There are realms of non-physical, high frequency parts of you, watching your back always. You have your higher self, inner being, intuition, whatever you wish to call the expanded part of you that guides you.

This mass ascension journey humanity is undertaking at this time has never been attempted in the universe before. You are watched with utmost love and eager anticipation by all the non-physical aspects of yourself as collectively we move towards such evolution and expansion. These are exciting times.

You came here for this. You knew you would undertake this journey, and you agreed to shine the light of

consciousness and to walk the path of self-actualization.
The light is available for all but only some are in the
vibration of receivership, and that is fine, all is well.
Don't get entangled in the divisions, for they are another
part of the illusion, and if you give it attention, you bring
more of it into your reality. Focus on the light and the love
and send it into the darkness and for the dark, for that is
enlightenment. Just hold steady in your resonance and as
you radiate light, more will gravitate to you, for that is law.
You knew it wouldn't be easy but you understood the
privilege to be here and be an integral part of this
ascension into heart-based living and the renunciation of
fear which is the very antithesis of who you are.
You came to create heaven on earth with your unity. You
are the wayfarers, and you came to push the limits of light
and dark. Now it is the time of light, as we all transition
away from division, discord, disharmony and back to love.

In our collective expansion, we will create through the
intention to radiate love. Stop for a moment and focus on
how that makes your heart feel. It has neuro-receptors
much like your brain, it is your heartfelt intelligence and it
has limitless capacity to project itself. Together we have
immense power through our mindful connection. Our
activation will create change from the dysfunctional into
the sublime.
Start seeing the meaninglessness of our current systems,
and imagine a world governed by the undercurrent of
love. Really think about it. Your thoughts create things.

Imagine and visualize everyone single soul safe and expanding.

People's hearts are awakening to this and the intrinsic knowledge that this is our time, this is our opportunity to make the world the wondrous place it has the potential to be. The light is spreading, the numbers of awakened hearts are growing exponentially, and we are thrumming like an avalanche to renew the landscape and rebuild a loving, thriving new earth.

This is ascension to the fifth dimension. All are going, no one gets left behind as that is not possible, though many are choosing to transition now and come back later after the process is complete. It is a time for transformation, to evolve you must change, it is the only truth, the only constant. You have experienced enough disconnection, it is now to time to experience full connection, a truly exciting time.
Imagine a physical reality of limitless creation with the full integration of consciousness in your physical body. This has never been done before, you are literally at the leading edge and jumping off point of new ways to exist in the physical body. Let your imagination run wild for a moment and you still can't fathom what you are capable of creating from full conscious awareness in physical form. Telepathy, energy manipulation, teleportation, astral projection, to be the consciousness of a soaring bird, the energy in an ocean wave, the vibration of a thought.

You may start to find that people, relationships, events and systems no longer resonate with your expanded frequency and fall out of existence for you. They are there and you know about them, they just don't show up in your reality anymore. Allow this, don't feel any guilt but permit the grief, feel it and release it and remember you are not and have never been responsible for someone else's choice about how they wish to experience this moment in their expansion. You are only ever a cooperative component in their life as they are in your yours.

As Shakespeare wrote "To thine own self be true and it must follow as the night the day, thou canst not then be false to any man." Smart guy.

However, the Universe abhors a vacuum, so that void needs to be filled with higher frequency systems, people, relationships and events. And that is what we are designing now. The New Earth, our Gaia a conscious being, evolving.
Tap into your sacred mind and unite it with your sacred heart and use the gifts you were born with, but were deactivated and ridiculed by the societies you grew up in. Share them with others so that more can be bestowed upon you, for the highest good of self and others. Envision your perfect world and allow spirit to nudge you towards it.

You are an electromagnetic being radiating an energetic charge. This charge can be measured to around a metre from your physical body, and that measurement is only because of the limited range instruments are capable of. Dr. Joe Dispenza uses them in his workshops.

You can re-programme your DNA with the vibration of your thoughts. (I have listed the scientists and research material available in the last chapters) check this mind-bending stuff out. If you are someone that needs to be told, the scientists will tell you, just be open to the new proofs if it is hard for you to feel it on your own. That is why this new science is happening, to give you something new to pull yourself towards as you let go of the old outdated models.

You are redefining this human experience through your evolving soul. These are epic times.

And you can create limitlessly, imagine your perfect world. No sickness, no aging, no lack.

Your human body is the most perfect technology ever. You are moving to full consciousness awareness within this physical body and in this lifetime, if you so choose it. Your body is literally the temple of your soul, the sacred place of connection for the superconscious to experience the material, how exciting is that, what a joy to be alive...!!!! You are a cosmic artist imbued with the creative gifts of the divine.

You are your own protagonist in this incarnation to serve your experience in any manner you wish. It is within this

incredible vessel that you engage the world and life.
Feel the full sensations of you not just loving life but life
loving you.

More energy is streaming in to planet Gaia and to us from
our sacred sun. Watch the effects on the Shumann
Resonance, which is the heartbeat and frequency of us as
a collective and our planet, Gaia. We are being assisted in
our ascension into the light. The purpose of this is to be a
fully integrated being of light in crystalline form. The full
embodiment of spirit. Limitless creation in physical. What
does that mean to you? Instant healing, the ability to
restructure your DNA at whim, breathe underwater? To
have the awareness that you are everything, to feel your
power in a thunderstorm, your stillness in a blade of grass,
your joy of being a wave before a particle. Seriously, take a
moment to think about this.
Imagine living in a joyous cohesive community with no
restrictions on invention, innovation and thoughts
becoming things. You might even wish to create challenge
so you can experience contrasts from which to create
something new.

This is a pivotal event, you are being shown that your
vibratory signature must be impervious to conditions. You
must accept your place in divine expansion and
understand that as you heal yourself, you heal your world.
You are an energy field radiating and the Law of Attraction
brings it all back to you, this is happening whether you are

deliberately creating or mistakenly creating by default. It is all you.

You are being offered an opportunity to remember. Your soul longs to see its essence radiating back, so be vibrant and fierce in your desire to heal the frayed connection to your Source from its attachment to illusion.

Humanity needs to value the creativity of life and start co-existing with consciousness.

You may find that you are experiencing unexplainable physical symptoms of ascension.

These can range from extreme fatigue, emotional triggering and mood swings. Aches and pains in specific areas of your body. Heightened awareness and senses. Headaches and ringing ears. There are probably more and some of the websites and groups listed at the end will reassure you this is normal.

Your physical body is being upgraded so you can literally embody the higher frequency energies of the higher dimensions. When your ears are ringing it is an energy recalibration on an interdimensional level. Once you know this, welcome and revel in it but practice self-care and awareness. Eat healthy whole foods, drink lots of water and rest. Remember that self-love is simply being attuned to your alignment and your vibration. You will know by how you feel, when you are out of the former, and low in the latter. When that happens become aware of why, maybe it is because of the people you are around, the thoughts you are thinking or the air you are breathing.

Whatever the cause, it is not serving you except to show you what tilts you out of alignment. Once you have that useful information, either take a nap, meditate or get into nature, walk or swim, to get back your high vibe.

Chapter 4

what you need to do

Accept and grasp wholeheartedly that no one and no thing is doing anything to you, life is not being perpetrated to you. You are not a piece on some gigantic chessboard, being moved around by some vengeful, punitive God. You are God.

All that you see and experience in your outer world is a reverberation of your inner world and the energetic signature that you are sending out. It is a perfect information feedback loop. Use it and the knowledge it provides you with, to understand where on the ascension ladder you are. You get to choose how you wish to progress. If you are not enjoying or expanding from what you are experiencing, you are the only one that can change it.

Everyone has an excuse to relinquish this responsibility, too much trauma, too much to identify with. A reason to blame. But once you take this path your life will become an expression of conscious joy, a work in miracles, a limitless expression of God.

Be committed, but be kind, this is not an easy road, but
the rewards are incalculable. Now is the time to apply
critical thinking and deep dive into you. It will take
dedication and commitment. You need courage, patience
and forgiveness.

The only questions now are
Who do you want to 'be'?
Where do you want to 'be'?
3D or 5D?

What were your dreams, passions and loves before they
were forgotten and pushed out by someone else's goals
for your life? What is it that makes living worthwhile for
you?
Apply yourself to the truth of your dreams. After lockdown
when you reassemble the splinters of your life, maybe
there is a different configuration that will fit better this
time, without the restrictions of opinion and expectation.
Perhaps you can embed the shards with love and throw
them to multiply on the wings of new opportunity. Set
love free in your new world. Let it invade everything with
liberation.

What would happen to your life, if when someone asked
you "how are you?" And you stopped complaining.
Remember the Law of Attraction. If you keep talking or
thinking about what you don't have, you will get more of
that lack.

Wonder what your lives would look like, if you existed in a state of appreciation for the miracles that occur every day. For the life that you are, to recognize the love that you are.
Say every day, "I love my life, I really love my life!" and see what happens instantly to your brain chemistry and then in your manifested moments.

Stop forgetting, start reconnecting with yourself, get your juices flowing, be the creator you are born to be. Innovate, design, paint, write, sing, play and most of all appreciate. Smile, laugh, touch, engage, remember how incredible you are and how loved and see what happens. Feel everything in the moment, for what do you need to be distracted by, really.
The fifth dimension is not a place or a destination. It is a state of being, a level of consciousness, it is oneness, gratitude, unconditional love, alignment. At times, during your daily lives, you visit there, when you hold a baby, hug your dog, watch a sunrise, make love. You are familiar with that feeling of peace and bliss, and it is from this vibration that you create the fortuitous events that you believe are luck or god given. You just haven't recognized the correlation. The fifth dimension is being in that state more frequently until it is your 'being' state.

The following paragraphs may seem a little harsh, but I write them with good intentions with the most love and kindness directed towards you as you absorb them. I want you to know that I have been where you are about to go, as many others have before you, and I promise you it is worth it. We are with you, energetically holding your hand and loving you so much for the courage you are showing in taking this step.

I have prostituted my soul in the shadowlands of insecurity, low self-esteem and self-respect, thinking it was fun at the time and convincing myself I was impervious to the secret knowledge of self-destruction and pious in the belief of self-sacrifice.

But eventually the delusion plays itself out and you are left only with the true gift of forgiveness for yourself and the life you deliberately manifested. Maybe it was my soul's journey, maybe it was on my soul's 'bucket list' of things to experience in human form. Whatever, it is done now, and I am blessed with the understanding of how unnecessary it is to feel that distortion for any longer than I wish to as I reach for a more in tune understanding of who I really am.

You are more than you think you are. And you are needed now, by those that went through this, are going through it and by our planet. Rise up, take the leap of faith. Take back your power. Have the resolution to seek your liberation in the truth of who you are. Be obedient only to this divine truth. Become integrity, become honour, become courage incarnate, then you will inspire others to find their own courage. This is revolution.

Why do you stay in prison when the door is so wide open –
Rumi

Maybe you are stuck in the lower dimensions of fear and
lack and have given up your right to free thinking by
choosing a divided aspect of self and limiting divisions of
race, tradition, religion, culture and looking for a
scapegoat.
Maybe you are waiting for solutions from the men in suits
in their skyscraper offices because you believe they have
this power. They only have the illusion of power. You feed
it to them with your helplessness and you buy it for them
with your will. Thus, you will always be waiting.
Maybe you believe that you are being made to suffer by a
condemnatory god that has never existed, except to
control you and stop you understanding that your true
power lies in love and unity.
Maybe you are entangled in the deceptive web of illusion
and density. Ego driven by either a self-centred
entitlement or a self-sacrificing complex of martyrdom, or
some variation in between. Allowing your anger,
bitterness, and blame to stifle and silence the continuous
torchlight of your soul calling you back home.

Your personality is not really you; it is an amalgamation of
traits that you project depending on what you hope to
gain from an encounter, a subconscious and unaware
trade off. This distorted transaction is unnecessary once
you realize that all that you encounter, without exception,

are responding to the energy you are projecting about how you feel about yourself. All responses will be entirely dependent on that fact alone. That is the mirror of creation. So, don't take who you think you are for granted or too seriously. Embark on a real excavation of discovery, dig deep in this exceptional opportunity for self-knowledge and self-mastery. This is why you are here, reading this book; you are tired of the same old, same old, you want a new adventure.

THIS is the greatest adventure you can ever decide to thrill to, it is a privilege of such magnitude. Your soul desires to watch and guide you as you start seeking the treasure that is you.

Release all your resistance, all your attachment to your perception of you and simply understand that you are the Universe evolving.

Some may find that they have a victim mentality and like to blame others or the world for the way they behave. This is a relinquishing of ownership and responsibility for life, but it allows martyrdom on a nonexistent altar. Some enjoy the attention they receive from drama, negativity and health issues. Unconsciously creating them to validate an existence that has never needed validation. Some choose the role of saviour, drawing victims to themselves in an ugly mismatch of co-dependency. An impossible vicious circle that goes on and on, as one tries to 'fix' and the other that can't be, by anything external.

Some give to others to make themselves feel better because they do not believe in their deserving of abundance. The gift then becomes corrupted. Be cautious as well about the message this sends. The implication may be "I give to you because I see you cannot give to yourself." It is a message of disempowerment and resentment is the only possible repayment.

Some of these truths are very hard to face and it takes courage and compassion. However, the whole needs all experiences to understand itself. You must experience what you are NOT, to understand what you are, it is why duality has been created. You have lived as the abuser as often as the abused. So, embrace it with the loving kindness it deserves, let it go and move on to the higher part of experience that is now opening up for you as a conscious creator standing in your full authentic power.

Let go of any attachment to trauma. Don't be so identified with your sad story that you repeat it again and again to anyone and thus, reaffirm your powerlessness. There is no need to prove your trauma was more than another's. There is no suffering scale for judgement. Let it go. It is just an event that you chose. You came with the intent to experience it, so you could know joy, compared to sorrow. That is all your pain is. Suffering, is wallowing in it, reliving it every time you speak it. Your subconscious does not know the difference between a memory and an

experience, it only knows the moment of Now, so as you
remember, so you feel again the trauma of it. Maybe you
have become addicted to the chemical reaction and so the
cycle repeats and repeats.
It is like stubbing your toe, and then deliberately,
continuously, banging it against a wall.
When you remember the bad times remember there was
good just beside it. When you tilted your face to the sun
and the warmth kissed your face, hours before your father
came home drunk and slapped it. Why do you not
remember the gentle love of Source and only focus on the
confused slap?
Stop protesting the past and what has transpired, it is
done. Acknowledge it, be grateful for it, it has revealed
your strengths to you. Release it as you move forward into
love. Let that loving momentum, define you.

Why drag your past with you as you fearlessly flow to the
blazing possibility of your future.

In the moment when you relinquish ego, even for a second
of stillness, you will feel a shaft of divine presence and you
will remember. When you stand in that immense power of
the full you, you realize that you are a gift of unfettered,
unimaginable love. There is nothing to lose and you can
give yourself to life unremitting and unchained from that
place of wholeness.

Be invincible in your vulnerability and your eternalness.

Your external and transient circumstances are nothing compared to the permanence and beauty of your inner knowing. Rather see what you have been blessed with. It is so easy to feel grateful when you have a mind to. You are reading these words, so you have sight. Think of all the beauty you have eyes to see. If you are holding the book, you have strength, probably also mobility, what a wondrous gift. Revel in it, touch something, make something, lift something, throw something.
Slough of the past, like on old worn skin, it no longer protects you, it is only shielding you from the truth of what you are. You are love. This is your natural state of being, you only move yourself away from this with habits of negative thought, it is that simple.
You become what you seek.
When you see yourself as worthy you will see the worthiness in others. You will have respect for others when you have respect for yourself.
Feel good and allow good, feel easy and allow ease, feel fun and allow fun. Feel inspired and allow inspiration. Follow the good feeling thought. Follow the goosebumps, follow the inspired action, follow the spontaneous impulse. It is your inner self guiding you forward on this blessed journey of remembrance and rediscovery of self.

It is your only work now, to release the addiction to self-sabotage, let go of limitation and distortion and stand in

your full authenticity. Claim every beautiful blessing, every gift and ability. The honour of empowerment. Revel in your abundant joy. Be the fun loving, cheeky one, the Universe created humour for. Receive it all, with open hearts and open arms, this incredible adventure of flow. Let the Universe show you with miracles, synchronicities and boundless joy what it can do for you with the raw creative power you have divine access to. It is your sovereign birthright. Claim it all right now, this instant. Define yourself in this magical moment of Now with your next cosmically conscious choice. Chose life, choose freedom from someone else's preconceived and constricting ideas. You are love made manifest in human form, embrace the miracle of you and allow the power that created the wonder of you into your life. Watch what happens, watch the expansion, watch the unmitigated abundance flow to you, when you manifest heaven on earth from the creative intelligence of your heart.
You have free will, and you can choose struggle and shackles or liberation and prosperity.
Change your story, change your perspective. Watch what happens when you exist in a state of gratitude. The energy of gratitude is the assumption that what you desire has already happened. That the gift has already been given. It is the most sublime receiving vibration.

Many people think it takes a long time to change, but that is just another belief system, you can redefine yourself with your next choice in this moment of Now. Remember, you are as powerful as the whole, you have the power that creates worlds at your fingertips.

Acknowledge your ego and what it is.
Your ego is survival based, it worries about the future and frets about the past. It loves labels and identities that it can assign to itself to allow it to feel safe and accepted by the crowd. It doesn't like change and will live in denial of patterns that clearly do not serve you anymore but give the ego something known that it can grasp onto. It is your sad story. Your drama, your attachment to the trauma of your past because it gets attention, validation and pity.
It loves the boxes that were created by someone's else idea or traditions that no longer apply to you. Your ego has an attachment to these labels because it is easy, there is no need to apply individual thought, which may make you stand out. You can just subscribe to the prevailing trends of the masses. This mainstream culture, which is often just a marketing ploy to get you to drink alcohol, buy certain products, watch television, and eat copious amounts of fat and sugar. Then the other companies can sell you the medication you will eventually need for your heart condition and diabetes. Your ego loves being fed bad news, as the fear engendered justifies its existence. As we move into expanded consciousness and heart-based living, the ego can now relax and let our intelligent hearts allow us to live from love instead of fear.
Your ego mind sees the world around you and analyses,

through logic and rationale and associations of the past, what it thinks it needs to do to ensure your survival and its own. It has only a limited perception with which to navigate through a world it deems as dangerous.

When your enquiring nature askes "What is the meaning of life, what is my purpose?" your blessed ego mind has not one clue. It is not equipped, so isolated it has become from its cohesion with the heart. It is only your heart that can answer this question, and it is only when the sacred mind is unlocked from its limitation through the reunion with the sacred heart, that the answers become clear.

Your sacred heart waits in eternal patience while you experience whatever life you choose without judgement. Just timeless, loving serenity until the moment is right for you to bring it online with attention and awareness.

When the twin flames of the sacred mind and sacred heart are brought back together, the light of you is fully conscious, cognizant and cohesive. This is divine expression, the awakening of the sacred love which is inherent in us all.

It doesn't have to be hard or painful. It is simply a recognition that you are tired of not telling your truth. All it takes is the renunciation of passive aggression and simmering resentment as it pollutes and drains you from the inside out.

Stand tall and say, "No, I don't believe that" or "No, I don't stand for that. Because to nurture myself and have honesty abound around me is more important than anything else, you, in your moment of distortion can ever offer me."

Remember the Law of Attraction has no favourites, it simply is and is responding to your offered vibration. Let go of your complaints and your frustration, irritation and pain. Move into appreciation and the full comprehension of your power as Source energy, able to bring into your physical reality whatever you want with ease and flow.

You will transform your life instantly as you start creating all the joy, money, relationships, fun and laughter you can ask for.

Doesn't this seem worth it?

What are you waiting for?

What are you scared of?

Are you afraid of more judgement? What's the difference from now except you will be far happier, energized and enthralled by your own life?

Filled with eagerness to create the next adventure.

The Universe is with you in your dreams, hopes and aspirations. It is right beside you as you explore your way to them. It wants to show you the way, guide you lovingly along a path of least resistance. Loving you whether you allow it access to its own creation or not.

The most debilitating belief you have been indoctrinated with is the fear of death and by proxy you have attributed that same belief to the people around you and your world. That it is a scary place and you can trust no one.

So you walk tentatively into your days, distrustful and wary, suffused with the expectation of hardship and tribulation, and so you create the very environment that you fear. Depressingly proving to yourself that you and they were right with their erroneous perceptions of a world that simply wishes to love you.

Until you redress this crushing fallacy you will blame the world, fate and a punitive god, when all life wants you to do is run joyously into life's open arms.

Stop wasting your time, stop wasting precious moments. Watch the children that haven't yet been corrupted by this lifelong shadow we are subjected to walk under. Watch them embrace the full rendering of life, as they revel in their own astonishment, the grass under their feet and in their mouths. Hugging the trees as they climb, sensing no divisions, talking to fairies and their imaginary friends, dancing under rain clouds as they welcome wonder. They expect miracles and they live life basking in its unconditional love.

You are as vast and deep as the world around you; doesn't that stop you in awe? Don't you think it is amazing? Bring it, I love it, I want it. I surrender to the higher part of me and move joyously forward in my evolution.

But bring me challenge, bring me variety and contrast as it is the mechanism through which I may grow, but I will not choose to suffer, I will not choose to stay there in complaint.

There is no need to prove strength, fortitude, resilience, to whom are you proving it to anyway. It is a waste of time, a waste of energy and a waste of this precious unrepeatable Now moment. All you need be is your soul's divine nature. Your proof is in the abundance of life flowing to you. The solutions that manifest from your attunement.

Do not get involved in criticism, drama and small-minded gossip. It lowers your vibration and just attracts more of the same. Do not be disheartened by the masses lost in the teachings of the unenlightened thoughtforms, habits and conditioning. Never forget that there are many paths back to oneness and all will find their way. It is not your role to convince, your role is as a warrior of light. Stay strong and gentle in your steadfast belief in your expanded reality. Show wisdom, and joyful acceptance of the wonder of life. Be the centred purveyor of your truth, for in such delightful expression, you will bring people to their own power by the forceful light of your own.
Imagine what your relationships would look and feel like. The expansion they would engender, if you could stand before another, knowing that whatever happens you cannot be diminished in your integrity and love. That they can stand before you, knowing that you know who they are. You will not judge their choices and you will never not love them. You understand they are you. This is freedom.

There is no 'good' or 'bad'. Everything just is. There is only perception that defines it so dependent on your belief systems, upbringing, experiences, relationships, race, gender etc. Ultimately, you can never know how or why someone judges something. But as you move towards understanding who you truly are, you realize that you are designing your own reality to learn, experience and create. Every event, encounter and episode, though named through your perception at the time as good or bad, is a gift you gave yourself to leisurely unwrap. To eventually define the lesson so subtle. To allow more growth and forward momentum towards this Now moment. Be grateful for each second of your story. You so beautifully created it in such perfection as to deliver you here, for the next expansion.

Be kind to yourself, forgive yourself for the emotions you feel, and the history you have lived. You are exactly where you planned to be, your journey is unfolding as you designed it to. All aspects of experience are required by the whole of you to know yourself. You and your life are an intrinsic part of an experiential journey, as essential as each other. Every single moment is loved and appreciated by All That Is, never forget this, hold this in your heart as your beautiful expansion reveals itself to you. Everything is as it needs to be, in divine order and you are a perfect being, in this perfect moment, always.

It is a spiraling process. Following a 'need to know' basis. Your reminders will come at exactly the right pace for you to incorporate the lesson.

As you move towards living as a fully conscious being, you must appreciate that it needs to unfold gently, as you

would overload your limited human understanding of
what is possible when you are completely aligned with the
whole. You would most likely implode with the influx of
energy and mind-bending information. Your physical body
needs to slowly attune to the higher dimensional part of
yourself. This is why many are experiencing symptoms as
they start integrating the new higher frequency energies
of spirit. It is the ebb and flow of ascension.

That is why this book is so repetitive, when the concept is
so simple.

I listened to Abraham Hicks all day, every day for eight
months until my ego mind would be quiet enough and
non-resistant enough for me to start accepting these
tenets.

Listen to Abraham Hicks yourself. Esther has been
repeating the same message for over 30 years. It is difficult
to absorb at first, because thinking as an indoctrinated
human, you can't believe you wouldn't make it harder for
yourself. You believe it should be more complicated and
there must be some form of sacrifice, that you must
paddle the boat upstream and you must work hard against
the flow to prove you deserve.

You, as a creator, know the blessed simplicity of continued
expansion. You were meant to observe something you did
not like and then create something better that you did.
That is the simplicity and beauty of evolutionary creation.

As you traverse up the lightpath out of density, you will find that many that travel alongside you, speak about resonance. This is a signal to you from the higher perspective part of you that something matches your innate energetic soul signature. It can manifest physically as goosebumps (sometimes called truthbumps) and feel like the eureka moment of epiphany. This resonance is important as it means you are on the right track.
You are an electromagnetic angelic song to a universe of vibration, frequency, cadence and tone. Resonance is harmony. As you move up out of the discordance of density, your soul sings, more vibrantly, your melody.

It is now that you understand that you change the world from within yourself first and foremost. In the reestablishment of your connection to your divine nature, you access that stream of intelligence, the fundamental river of life, the unified field of information, where all possibilities exist. With awareness and incorruptible love, you can change the nature of reality and choose your next experiences. You can now recreate with bold ideas. You now become the pioneer as a warrior of spirit with new vision.
What will you choose Now?
What will be your legacy?
Will you guide by example, share your insights, become a teacher or a practitioner or simply be the one that says "I will always choose happy over right. I will live without care of your opinions. My only goal is to infinitely and

incessantly live the full expression of me, in the full expression of life."

The Ultimate Truth

Feel your heart, focus on the space in your chest where you heart dwells, feel its expansion, feel its willingness and desire to fill you with ecstatic appreciation of all that you are. It is a vast infinite supply of what you are made of. It wants to be released and exploded out to encompass everything and all.

It is when this love is suppressed or based on expectation and need, that it hurts us. We have been made to mistakenly believe, that withheld love is a shield that protects us. Or that it requires repayment for us to be completed. This backwards thinking is destroying us all. We need to change this fallacy as we realise the damage we inflict with denied, conditional love.
We cripple ourselves when we make love a currency.
All of us painfully ache to feel safe enough to love. But we need to release these inexhaustible reserves of eternal love, and then there will be safety for all.
Your love of self makes you incorruptible and indestructible. Unconditional love is where your true power lies.
This is your inherent superpower. Go, wield it with courage, indiscriminately and in its purity.
Everything responds to love.
You are the inviolate simplicity of everlasting love.

Chapter 5

why you need to do it

Create the life of your dreams through the application of this knowledge.

YOU are the star of your movie.

Reality is subjective to you.

You have chosen your parents, your upbringing, your ethnicity, sex, social status, disabilities, wealth, health issues, children, life experiences and death.

Remember that there is no 'death' you are an eternal being of pure conscious awareness/energy, there is only transition.

There is no illness or sickness, there is only dis-ease. Your body is built to function in perfect harmony with its surroundings. What you put into it, whether polluted air, chemically infused water, or brutalized food, will have a harmful effect. You need the higher frequency energy of your state of being to transmute it. You will be as healthy as you expect to be. Illness is just a reminder that you are far from your optimum emotional state of being. You are far away from the homeostasis that the physical vessel was designed for. In other cases, you either came here to experience pain and suffering, or it is part of yours or another's awakening process. So learn the lesson, let it go and move into higher experiences.

If you have been told that you have a high chance of contracting a disease, and you spend the majority of your time worrying that you will, then you will most likely suffer from it. You will attract it to you by your focus upon it. Repressed anger or a life inauthentically lived, creates enough discord to create dis-ease. Eating away the inside of you spiritually and then physically through the manifestation of illnesses that do the same. These are difficult truths to accept, but once accepted you can move into a fully conscious expression of self and be the integral part of your own healing. Do your own research into the science of Dr. Bruce Lipton and modalities such as Quantum Healing Hypnosis Technique - QHHT™ listed in the back of this book.

You are a creator, and the physical plane is the best realm for the direct visceral sensation of experiencing your manifestations. Not only can you touch, taste, smell, see and hear them you also have an emotional reaction to them.

All emotions like everything else have a vibrational frequency that range low to high on a scale. Starting at the bottom with dense negative emotions like hatred, anger, bitterness, shame, guilt etc and moving up to neutrality in the middle, to acceptance, love, joy, gratitude and bliss at the higher end. You are aware of how each one makes you feel physiologically, your racing heart, and your trembling hands etc. Whichever emotion you are feeling you are radiating it out, not just to affect your manifested reality, but also out to the collective conscious so that it effects our global manifested reality.

As a collective, we have become more disconnected, negative, judgmental and critical. We have moved so far away from the heart of our Source and lost ourselves in the painted false reality of control, fear, limitation and separation. We have cut ourselves off from the unifying love we all seek. This has affected our world. We have war, inequality, chaos and division. We have forgotten our connection to our planet, creating her misuse.

Our planet has a name, Gaia and she is a conscious being. As preordained by her alone, she is ascending into the fifth dimension and she encourages all that wish, to join her.

In the Fifth dimension, low frequency and density cannot exist. You decide Now whether you would like to assist with the ascension process or stay in density.

Gaia, as she ascends will start to slough off the negative trauma that has been perpetrated along her pristine shores, spectacular mountains, forests, oceans and deserts. She is rebalancing and reharmonizing her energy system. Her crystalline diamond core and golden gridlines are being reactivated from the dormant low-density energy that we, over millennia, have infused into her with our destruction and disconnection.

This is why there are such massive changes in the weather patterns. The reemergence of animals into their original habitats before they were edged out by our thoughtless rampage.

Gaia, and those of you that chose, are realigning. This is not something to fear, it is your destiny as you move into awareness and resonance with your divine nature and rebalance with your Mother Nature. All you need to do is take notice of her and her sublime beauty. Her harmony and balance and include yourself in her infinite grace.

Look at the plant on your windowsill, inhale the sweet fragrance and see the fractal patterns of the whole on its leaves. Understand that it too, is conscious and responding to your vibration as clearly as if you blow it a kiss or smack it with a baseball bat.

Listen to the birds, the morning chorus which is a declaration of love from the expanded part of you. Feel the grass beneath your feet, gently caressing and holding you solidly as was the promise from an eternity ago. Never forgotten as you have been held and supported through your struggle and misdirection.

Look at your oceans and water ways and feel the energy that runs through your fingers as well as the life supporting liquid. How it feels to be submerged, diving through waves, like diving through portals into serenity. How did you forget and why? It does not matter now. All that matters, in this perfect moment, is that you understand that you can make a different choice. You can redefine yourself with your next choice, you can elevate your vibration in the next moment of Now. Right Now, right Now. Remember connection and alignment is not something you get done, and then it is finished, and you can buy the t-shirt, it is a state of being, continuously and consciously. It is your divinity.

The Corona virus was a gift to us, by us, because in our 3D mentality of non-appreciation of the moment, we often only realize what we have when it is gone. We were happily wrecking our planet and slowly annihilating ourselves. Our souls were crying out for us to stop. Stop living in such haste, running from pillar to post. Chased down by fears, bosses, opinions, judgements, lack, corporations, marketing schemes, disillusion, and disappointment.

Collectively we shut ourselves away, so we could reemerge with remembrance.

Don't waste this gift.

Look to the sunrise, the clouds, the birds, the trees, the green hills and valleys, the imposing mountains, forests and oceans. Our animals and beasts so perfectly designed to be aesthetically pleasing to the eye. This gentle solace of love so pure, the intricately spun web of symbiosis so graceful in its complete perfection.

Feel the sun on your face, the gentle breeze that ruffles your hair, the ants across your path, the bird on your front gate, the squirrels in your trees. KNOW in your heart that each is the highest form of unconditional love, a gift to show you your pathway home, the light you left on for yourself.

Always calling you,

"Hey I am right here, look up, listen, just stop for a moment and feel my natures breath inside you, breathing with the same cadence and rhythm as you. We are one, you and I, and I have never left your side, come back to unity and grace, let's be light again once more. You have been gone too long dear one, come back and let's ride our river together."

"Come outside with the fresh air in your lungs and the early morning sun on your face, let me revitalize you, allow me to be absorbed into your being, allow me to share my heart with yours, just stop and feel me within you.
Don't turn away, let my love overwhelm you and resuscitate you. Feel infused by it, let it permeate through you and out and around you. I am, you are, life. Let me flow through you."

Ask yourself if there really is anything more important than feeling like this in any given moment.? I ask you to take a moment, stop and feel.
We didn't come here to tame nature, it's impossible and, thankfully we failed miserably. We came as a team to live in harmony together. Look at the laws of Mother nature, how perfectly balanced she is and see how they also apply to us, as a collective. We must embrace them to thrive together.
We need collaboration, and we need diversity as it allows for adaption and resilience. We need to understand our interconnectedness as we effectively use our resources,

mindful of consequences and take responsibility for our actions.

Do you really think you came here to blindly follow someone else's idea of how to live this precious life of yours? Relinquishing your power to their rules and doctrines, subjected then, to their restrictions, judgements and opinions. Remember in your teenage years rebelling against a system that didn't make sense to your soul, and then your eventual submission. To then start running around, trying to look busy in a desperate attempt to validate your existence.

Are you living in denial of your responsibility to embrace this sacred gift of life?

Now is the time that you change those systems. Now is the time to allow consciousness to participate in its own creation. The only way to start this change is from within, for as you connect more fully to the higher part of you, your choices become based on oneness and not separation. That is the fundamental difference between third density existence and fifth density living. You could call the fourth density the transition from the 3D to the 5D, it is a state of question, wonder and openness. It is a tacit acknowledgement that if you are not moving forward, you are stagnating, and energy trapped stays dense. It is you, following your hearts guidance towards full heart-based living. Out of fear and into the flow of love.

There are 7.8 billion human realities being lived on planet Earth/Gaia right now. Obviously, you have cooperators in this game, your friends and spouses, children etc, but they are each living their own perspective of reality. Together though we do have a collective consciousness that we are all connected to, and this is what is helping to speed up our awakening. As more and more of us start looking at evolution for ourselves and our souls, the more we stop giving energy, whether positive or negative, to that which no longer serves us. These disabling constructs then start crumbling as they have nothing with which to sustain them. Ever wondered why the media wants you focused on fear, inequality, scarcity and stress, it is like an energy feed for the outdated and power-hungry control structures in place today. As we start moving our focus to equality, abundance, love and kindness, these systems will collapse, and that is what we are seeing happening now, in real time. Collectively the quicker we each start to awaken, exponentially the quicker the awakening will happen. The old ways are falling, they are bankrupt anyway, for us to build the heart-based systems that will replace them. Systems where ALL are safe, no child goes to bed hungry, scared, neglected, abused. No parent need worry about how to keep their child housed, fed and clothed. Every sentient being is respected and cared for. Understand now that YOU are the only ONE. And that which you do unto another you do unto yourself.

This is the truth that will set you free. This is the purity and grace of you. Your majestic essence.

Chapter 6

How you do it

Examine your belief systems. Everything in your life reflects your beliefs, about yourself, and the world around you. These beliefs are just habit of thought. They can be constructive or destructive. Your beliefs in institutions, governments or anything external coming to save you, is giving your creative energy away and is just more attachment to division.

These are someone else's thoughtforms. Expunge them all.

The only belief you should have is the belief in oneness. You are the totality of all, and therefore everything else is. So, to do harm to another, is to do harm to yourself. There is only You.

You have been kept from the true understanding of how powerful you are. You are weakened when you are scared and confused. And that is where the media and the big corporations want to keep you. You are so easily controlled when you look externally for solutions, in their antidepressant pharmaceuticals, stimulants and alcohol.

Or brainwashing programming on your screens.
They don't broadcast the enriching messages, or the science that proves we are one. The quantum entanglement that connects us all. They marginalize and ridicule, or call new age, the scientists that show the old ways are wrong. Do your own research, there is incredible proof and research out there. Make your move from acquiescence and ignorance into empowerment and awareness.

Do not immerse yourself in the deluge of fear, those that wish to control you, try to drown you with.

Read books like this, have a look at the lists of books at the end of this one. Find likeminded people and have inspiring conversations that involve ideas and solutions. Listen to uplifting music and watch heartening and educational programmes. Stop watching the news, get into nature, listen to the birds and the rustling of energy. Explore, swim, climb trees, learn an instrument, play, do rollypolly's down the garden. Watch Lionel Messi play football, you play football.

Stop thinking that you must do something you don't want to do. This is a belief handed down and drummed into you by people and organizations that want to control you through fear and a belief that they need you to act a certain way for them to be happy. That is the definition of selfish. Most don't even know how or what will make them happy, so how are you supposed to know. If you can figure it out (impossible) then they don't have to. If you can't (likely) then they can blame you for their unhappiness. Think about that, read that again, does that make sense to you? You are pushing the boulder up the never-ending mountain of someone else's expectations. The only way you can help someone find their alignment is to be staunch and unwavering in your own. Show them, through your love and abundance, that they can find their way, through their own heart, to their own empowerment. Be the beacon of light that shines forth in the darkness, for people to see their way to.

You are not responsible for the change in anyone else, but you can inspire that change through your example.

Observational Gifts

The world changes from love-based choices.

You will stop eating industrially farmed animals when you can no longer stomach the brutality you put them through.

You will stop injecting stuff into your face that has been tested on animals, when you understand you are already beautiful.

You will stop buying items made in child labour slave shops when you understand those children are you.

You will stand for peace caused by your abhorrence of war

and the knowledge that the lessons are already learned.
Negative emotion is not wrong it is just guidance.
You can focus on the solution from the vibration of
fairness, instead of the problem from the vibration of
unfairness.
Don't look at the trash on the beaches and in the parks
and feel anger. Acknowledge that the person that dropped
it is not coming back to pick it up. The council is not going
to clean it as the money has been stolen by corrupt
officials. Each one is You anyway. Be proactive in the
cleaning up and reach for the fulfillment of creating
something better.
Make choices that build you, not break you.
There is no punishment and no judgement. There is only
expression and evolution. Your power is within you, has
always been, you are a being of light, a being of immense
information. So, smile without restraint, glow without
shyness, radiate your miraculous, love infused heartbeat.

Feel your heart, feel its expansion of love and hope
declared loudly and vibrantly for all to see. Bless every
moment of Now with your joy, see what happens when
every moment is blessed with happiness and boundless
glee, for life IS.
Be without apology, without conformity, without
hesitation.
Dance with the Universe in this beautiful description of
your life and live each moment in humble and joyful

appreciation of its magnificence.

You have come this far in the book, you know who you really are, why you are here, what you need to do and why you need to do it.
Accept your mission and the quest for self-mastery. Accept full responsibility of the unfolding creation of life. Let go of belief systems, thought patterns, patterns of behavior and your attachment to doctrine and your diminished self. Be your authentic true self, radiate it out, be unequivocal, unrelenting in the honour you feel to be you. Let your staggering self-acceptance be the light that others can follow and therefore allow their own transformation. That is the gift you bring. Face and discard your self-lies and speak your truth. Take your power back. Claim and accept your divinity and sovereignty. Spread it though your passion and integrity and fearless joy of who you truly are.

You raise your vibration when you meditate. Try, each day for 15 minutes or so to quiet your mind and silence the chattering ego of scattered thought.
It is no prayer; it is communion with the higher aspect of yourself. When you are still enough to listen, you will hear the guidance from the raw creative energy that swirls within you. It will come as an impulse, an urge, an inspired thought. Get ready to follow it, you are crazy if you don't, you are crazy if you don't stop to listen.

Being in alignment means you are always connected to your Source. Life flows, your intuition guides you. You know you are not alone and have never been. You focus on solutions and innovation to solve problems. You are aware of the beauty and perfection around you, synchronicities and ease, flow. You are in a heightened sense of appreciation as the world unfolds around you in magical and mystical ways, and you expect as much. You find you attract people that think the same way, and your connection is deep as both of your inner selves see each other as you truly are.

There are two ways to know what your energetic vibration is,

1) by how you are feeling

2) by what you are manifesting (experiencing) in your life. We have been provided with a map and GPS system to stay in alignment and not stray too far from the path. But we have always had free will. So much free will that we could choose suffering, but we would always have our guidance system calling us back to the path of alignment. You can readjust accordingly.

There are only two states of being:

Either you are in alignment with Your Source energy, inner being, higher self, broader perspective part of you, expanded consciousness, Soul. Or you are being called back to it through your emotional GPS system.

You are either calibrating to Source energy or you are manipulating those around you to get the transient illusion of it.

You are either in the perfect void of the Now moment or you are trying to fill that void with addictions of action, the roles you have labeled yourself with, or drugs and drink. So many people are looking externally for validation, running around and trying to prove worthiness through continued action. A human 'doing', they need others to respect them, love them, follow them, listen to them. This reaction is needed for them to have a sense of self. Another person struggling on their own journey cannot do this with any consistency, so both are left continuously trying to prove something they do not need to prove, to an external source that doesn't exist.

You are making your internal state of being dependent on external conditions and circumstance. For example, when you have that job, that lover, that car, you will be content and satisfied. The Universe does not work like that. You need to choose to feel delight first, then you will attract more things that make you delighted. You need to be able to say to those around you.

"I do not need or expect you to make me happy, I take full responsibility for my own happiness. But bring your happy and match it with mine and we can be fearless in our joy. I will look at you in your integrity and authentic alignment and you will be overwhelmed by the fierce purity of my love. For in my alignment I will be looking at you with the unconditional love of Source."

Once you realize this, all your relationships will be

uplifting, for you will understand the true nature of each other. This is what Namaste means, "The divine in me sees and recognizes the divine in you". Stand in your authenticity and set clear boundaries. In these relationships, unmediated anger cannot exist. Neither can unconscious reactions that accomplish nothing but a more divergence from self.

You are in alignment when you feel good. When you are doing the things you love and engaged in your passions. Watching a sunrise, in a cuddle puddle with your pets, moving down through the gears of your car as you sublimely take a corner, a warm hug etc. You KNOW when you are in alignment as it just feels so amazing...!!!

Choose to be the guiding light in how to exist, truly. Be the one that has never felt convinced of this dense reality and its weird belief patterns, and in that measure of uncertainty find your own alignment. Continuously show the way through compassion and gentle guidance for others. You may be the one that needs to rise, so that your family and friends can raise their hearts to the light that you shine so bright from your own.
As they say, don't be part of this current paradigm, be the one to connect to those that are changing it. Help people individually and collectively navigate their way through the dark night of the soul.
Be the one that has an innate understanding of the wonder, that each is a part of the whole. The universe is

exploring itself through limitless variance. Uplift others to see themselves as the pure positive energy that they are. Allow forgiveness for all, through the higher part of yourself and through which you can expand and enrich your experience through connection. Never underestimate the power of humility, compassion, gratitude and kindness. See everyone with a resonant understanding that each of us are a divine light of grace, and live your life intuitively, supremely guided by infinite love itself.

Activate within you your desire for true knowledge of self.

Trust your intuition and inner guidance. If a thought fills you with inspiration, a lightness of being, an impulse to action that you can't help but be spurred by, then it is your inner wisdom coming from your super conscious awareness and you are blessed.

Join the legions of light, radiating love. Lifting. It is time to fly, you are an angel becoming. Integrate the light. The changes are happening on a subatomic level, you are being infused with the light of creation.

If you are reading this book and it is engendering any awareness, I am very grateful. This means the information within is resonating with you. Your vibration is rising and you are radiating high frequency energy out, which is, quite literally, in this moment, changing the world around you, and for us.

It is important to note, though, that I didn't write it, it wrote itself through me. This is what happens when you are in flow with your divine nature, this is what happens when you release your attachment to your ego mind and your attachment to outcome, life just joyously flows through you. Just watch Lionel Messi play football, that is pure alignment in dynamic flow.

To become aware of how wonderful your life is, write a list of at least 100 things that you love. These are some suggestions,
the sound of your dog eating,
the smell of your lovers skin,
the colour of the sky at twilight,
the softness of your babies skin,
when your dog winks at you,
the heat when someone's arm is around you,
the sound of your car starting when you turn the key,
the compression of a good heart felt hug,
the vast feeling in your heart as you watch the ocean or the star filled sky.
Write them all down. Feel the feeling of each one, imagine it as you write it, feel the smile on your lips, the crinkle at the corner of your eyes and the expansion in your heart. This is the fifth dimension. This feeling is what you are looking for, it is why you think you want all the external physical, material things. The lover, the car, the pots of money, but you can have this feeling now, in this moment, you don't need the external conditions. When you feel like

this, think to yourself "this is how my higher self feels all the time, watching me create"
Don't turn away or close your eyes to the wonder of us.
Love life as the reflection of yourself, make it your most astounding artistry.
Smile, it changes your body chemistry instantly.
Slide and skate across a supermarket floor.
Have a trolley race across the carpark.
Be silly, play games
Watch screaming goats on YouTube.
Laugh, but not at the humiliation or pain of others.
Have a food fight, bury a friend in soft warm sand.
Play Twister™, drunk or sober.
Dance with abandon, sing loud.
Let go of what no longer serves you.
Simplify your life and surroundings.
Leave obligations you don't like.
Don't make promises you can't keep.
Speak up, say no.
Be who the universe knows you to be.
Stand and comprehend you have the power that creates worlds at your back and in your fingertips. Envision lightning bolts of supreme, unmitigated creative power shooting from your palms. Do not underestimate who you are and what you are capable of. Become it, be it, become more in each moment.
What could you be afraid of, failure? This is not possible.
Responsibility? Then you are only allowing mediocrity.

The judgement of others? Is that how you choose to define yourself?

There is so much information out there, it begins with you, with one choice, with one tentative or bold step on the path. Will you do the research? You have access to so much information that ignorance is also a choice.
It is an unequivocal fact that the Universe is quantum in nature. That You are made of subatomic waves of energy. Conscious, intelligent, energy. It has been known for a while, but it is not mainstream information, and you may have to dig a little for it and put aside your own cognitive dissonance.
It is not mainstream because it does not fit the narrative, perpetrated by those that use your powerlessness against you for their own twisted need of your control and subjugation. They want you wandering aimless through their days of dominance. All institutions from religions to governments want you cowering in fear and dependent on their authority. But the information is there, and the truth will set you free.
Do not abdicate yourself from the responsibility of taking your power back, to create the life you want to experience in this exceptional incarnation. As you raise your vibration and your higher thoughtforms express in your reality as manifestations of true community, you rise in your oneness to allow love to be your governing principal.
Start doing your own research, Google the names at the end of this chapter, watch their YouTube channels, read

their books and find the one that presents the information in a way that resonates with you.

They all present the same information, for these tenets are the keys to the kingdom of self. They just do it in their own special and unique way. Find the one you like, and binge watch them. Some have had past traumatic experiences that brought to fruition their awakening and this you may relate to. There is no bias in the way this information is expressed. Brainwash yourself with this empowering information before others do it with their twisted abortive logic and disempowering control mechanisms.

You become what you seek.

What are you looking for? Reasons to fear or reasons to cheer.

Dream big, dream bold, envision and imagine the abundance of energy flowing through you to create only what benefits all. For the highest good of all. Power if up, fuel your dreams with love. What then will your legacy be?

You can only be the love that you claim as your own.

You can only project from you, the love that you recognize you are.

We need each other as artists, look at Ronaldo and Messi, they love each other but some reporters depict their rivalry harshly. We are led to believe this is what

competition against each other should look like,
meanwhile it is a lie. We need others to inspire and
challenge us, to bring out the best of us. We are the
architects, in the throes of revealing our creative potential
in our unique ecstasy of expression.

You are everything

You are the warmth of a babies breathe
You are the swish of a dogs happy tail
You are the energy of love emanating, everywhere
You are the fluttering wings of the Hummingbird
You are the turbulent wind beneath them
You are the ray of sunlight on your pillow
You are the immense heat of the Sun
You are the soft breeze on your face
You are the inky vastness of the night sky
You are the space between
You are the smile of a stranger
You are the caress of your lover
You are the explosion of Wasabi up your nose
You are the thermal the Eagle soars on
You are the Eagle
You are the wave as it tumbles to shore
You are the shore tumbled upon
You are my inspiration, as you are my momentum and you
are loved beyond measure.

To illustrate the collaborative power of the Universe. The writer of this book has a deep desire to build a children's academy. The belief in its manifestation is as strong as the desire. When these are a vibrational match, the whole power of the universe starts amassing the cooperative components to start making it come to fruition in your physical reality. This book is written with inspired action, in alignment with the vibration of the energy that spins galaxies. It may well be the path of least resistance for the money to be generated for the school. If you have bought this book, you are part of the cooperation that will result in the construction and manifestation of that school.

Now is time to focus our expanding understanding and levels of consciousness and look to new ways of being and co-existing in harmony with each other and our environment. A time to move to collaboration and community, where individual skills and talents are brought together for the creation of projects designed in balance with Nature that benefit all.
As the old outdated systems crumble, we are guided to co-create the new world with a completely different set of affirming values and ways of living. We are creating our New Earth, now.
The aim is to provide a children's home/academy and animal sanctuary. Where orphans and disadvantaged children can be housed in safety. Teaching the children to discover and embrace their limitless potential and innate gifts that come from loving, focused intention and

attention.

Likeminded people, living from their hearts, vibrating at the same frequency. A support network built on a framework of love, service, compassion and caring, uplifting each other to higher and higher levels of consciousness. We will home the lost, unwanted, forgotten and neglected and show them their capacity for healing and their unlimited potential through unwavering heart-based living. A place where everyone is safe, unconditional love is the baseline of interaction and each is inspired to keep reaching for the highest potential of self. To embrace the exciting challenge of continuous expansion, evolution and connection.

Ultimately, those involved believe that when all are encompassed in an environment of serenity, trust and infinite love. Encircled by the connection to divine nature and respect of her harmonious symbiotic systems and energetic exchange. Where days are filled with laughter, connection and fun. Surrounded by people defined by love and personal truth. Committed to growth and expansion, through intuitive heart-based guidance, and not restricted by outdated and limiting beliefs. This will allow everyone access to their innate skills and inherent abilities of manifestation, communication with nature, telepathy, energy manipulation, third eye and intuition activation, healing and more.

When you have chosen this path of self-discovery and

have committed to your own self-mastery. You will find others. Your soul tribe and your soul family will be drawn to you as your interconnectedness becomes apparent. You will feel them in your inspiring conversations and desire to explore possibilities and new solutions.

You will need each other as you start living experiences that are more than what you are used to. As your ability to adjust your perception to the reality that you know is there, crossing the quantum threshold, you will start to see life the way your higher self sees it.

Time spent in self-practice and self-reflection will attune you to the energy around you. Through Qi gong, and other energy manipulation practices you may start to see or sense the energy, and then move it. You do this in a meditative state of complete alignment and with focused intention. At first it is so subtle you can barely feel it, but your sensitivity will become stronger until you can see it, feel it and sense it. Continuous practice will eventually develop gifts beyond just your intuition. These can be one or many or all or none of the following abilities:

Clairvoyance (inner or clear sight)

Clairaudience (inner or clear hearing)

Clairsentience (inner or clear feeling)

Claircognizance (inner or clear knowing)

Clairalience (inner or clear smelling)

Clairgustance (inner or clear tasting)

The above Clair senses are sensing abilities that are beyond the five physical senses, of sight, hearing, touch, taste and smell.

There are also the gifts of seeing energy in auras and in Gaia's gridlines etc.

Manipulating energy, as in healing and opening chakras and portals. There is no limitation to what we can do and infinite possibilities that I can't list.

You are capable of such magic when you allow, accept and believe. Stop the unfocused, manipulated thoughts of your ego mind. Open your valve and let the energy of Source to flow to you and through you. It is a process that requires practice and patience. It must be this way otherwise your mind would explode or shut down as it is just too much information to assimilate in one shot. Permit the unfolding at its perfect pace, and trust. But be diligent, apply yourself, follow the processes, do the research. Education and application are fun anyway.

Eat healthy foods, drink lots of water, and bless them before you consume them.

Think good thoughts and watch your positivity effect your world.

Set a morning Intention to be aligned with your higher self and choose only things for your highest good. Ask for a protective shaft of white light to shine down on you as you venture forth in this human body. You are giving permission to your higher self, to guide, inspire and direct you. Ask to strengthen your connection through your intuition as you make decisions that create only harmony, balance and beauty in your life.

Start telling a new story, filled with joy, abundance and appreciation. Enrich the world by shining your light from within, feel how much power there is in humility and gratitude.

Have no judgement for there is utter beauty in each individual variance, but know each as pure positive energy and treat them as such.

Stop watching the news, it is a program to keep you in fear and confusion.

Turn your TV off, you don't need disconnected entertainment.

Get into Nature.

Listen to Mei-lan Mauritius.

Find stillness for 15mins a day.

Write down seven things a day you are grateful for.

Be thankful and say so before you eat a meal and for each day, before you go to sleep.

Stop buying stuff you don't need.

Shop at second hand or charity stores.

Give stuff you don't need to charity.

Stop giving energy to trauma and drama, it doesn't need to exist in your new, chosen reality.

Go to the animal shelters and visit with them, volunteer to take them for walks.

Visit the elderly in care homes.

Volunteer.

Clean your local beach, park, nature walk, car park.
Pay more attention to your own family members.
You will start to find fulfillment and satisfaction and
expansion.
These are good ways to raise your vibration, open your
heart chakra and move from service to self to service to
others.

Every teacher listed, will speak about meditation and how
it is an integral part of the connection process. This book is
no different. Meditation is the quickest and simplest way
to connect to your divine nature. The quickest way to
silence your preconditioned mind and listen to your
unconditional heart. It is where the answer to all your
questions live. It is where you will experience oneness. It
will give you the real-time experience of what you are
surrendering to and for.
The feeling of divine oneness will encapsulate and pervade
your body, mind and spirit and you are left with no doubt
about who you really are. You are the I AM in the present
everlasting moment of Now, and it is magical.
Anyone can meditate, old or young, fit or feeble, sick or
healthy, rich or poor. Regardless of colour or religious
affiliation and doesn't that fact in and of itself, prove an
intelligent consciousness. You literally do not have to do
anything but stop the thoughts in your head and care
enough to listen. You only need to do it for 15mins a day,
and you can find that. I urge you to make the effort, it is a
step on the path to everything that you desire. It is the

only thing missing in your life that will satisfy you and bring you to wholeness.

You in your human form don't believe anything exists that you can't perceive through your five senses, you wouldn't believe in a Wi-Fi signal until I gave you a mobile phone and connected you to the internet. So, you need to start feeling. You need to start believing before you start seeing. You didn't come here to suffer, you came here to create through the energy of your thoughts, intentions and emotions.
There is so much information out there for you to seek the evidence of this if you find it difficult to switch from your limited ego mind, to your limitless heart.

To start your journey into research and education. Look at Dr. Joe Dispenza, Dr. Bruce H Lipton PhD, Gregg Braden, Wim Hof and Lynne McTaggart. I recommend reading their books, watching their videos on YouTube and attending their workshops. Their research is the link between science and spirituality and will offer you tangible proof of the intangible.

Dr. Joe Dispenza has studied neurology, neuroscience, brain and memory function, quantum physics, chemistry, cellular biology, aging and longevity. His book 'Becoming Supernatural' is an easy to understand, step by step guide to unlocking unlimited human potential. He uses state-of-the art technology to measure brain waves, individual energy fields and heart coherence at his workshops to show that meditation and focus increase our innate self-healing and manifestation abilities. His technology also shows that you have an energy chakra system. His meditation for the blessing of these energy centres, shows how to revitalize your aura and what a harmonious chakra system looks like. Watch him on YouTube as he talks us through the piezoelectric effect of the pineal gland. It is a transmitter and a receiver. Think about that. To what are you transmitting and from what are you receiving?

Dr. Bruce H. Lipton is a biologist at the forefront of the science of Epigenetics. From studying cell biology and quantum physics, he helps you understand how your cells process genetic information, and why, within our DNA blueprint our genes are switched 'on' or 'off' depending on our environment and our beliefs. His book 'Biology of Belief' describes how we can see the full potential of the human mind and its effect on our cells.

Gregg Braden is a scientist, researcher and author of many books that bridge science and spirituality. From the Mayan calendar to the fractal nature of galaxies and leaves. He explains the intricate beauty of the Universe in simple language, deeply researched. Watch him on YouTube as he explains the intelligence of the heart and that it has its own sensory neurites that allow it to think independently of the brain. His research on the lost gospels of Thomas, show that the knowledge of consciousness, oneness and manifestation were removed from the bible texts during the edit of Constantine in 325AD.

Lynne McTaggart is one of the central authorities in the new science of consciousness. Her studies and experiments into the power of intention have led to numerous books that detail how this powerful connection works. 'The Intention Experiment' and 'The Power of Eight' illustrate that the intense focus, of minds and hearts in coherence, can cause life-changing transformation.

Wim Hof backed by extraordinary and groundbreaking science, can teach you how to access your inner physiological power to heal and regulate your body. His three pillars method is the foundation for the evolution of your physical human potential.

Nassim Haramein is a physicist. Watch his YouTube episode on 'The Physics of Spirituality' where he explains that reality is a vibrational information feedback loop.

Arvin Ash explains quantum physics and the amazing nature of our Universe in easy to follow YouTube videos. Watch his episode on the 'Delayed Choice Quantum Eraser'.

Chapter 7

This Way Up

Just to reiterate and make sure you have understood the single message this book conveys.

Everything is energy, which vibrates at different frequencies. Nothing can exist which is not composed of this energy. This is pure primal energy and it is conscious, aware, intelligent. It is inexhaustible, incorruptible, a limitless energy field of unmanifest potential. That is what you are. You are composed of love, the intrinsic nature of god and you are endowed with such immense power which is your inherent sovereign birthright. Once you accept that all is energy including you, that there is no separation, division, distinction or difference, then you are in communion with spirit. Become its declaration.

You have within you the original divine blueprint, you are god made manifest, accept your divine dynamic power. Wield it with cosmic love, in the infinite present, the creative moment of Now as it is all that exists. Make your vibrational set point, unconditionally happy and see what happens in your life.

Live from your intelligent heart and your sacred mind within your incredible physical body. Your thoughts are electric, your emotions are magnetic. You are a field of electromagnetic energy radiating out from your body. You influence everything. You are everything. You are creating everything including the expansion of the All.

The Chakra System

You are an energy being, composed of energetic lifeforce. You have a charge of energy running through you. Sometimes called prana, chi, the force, Source energy.

Throughout your energy being, you have energy vortices. Portals through which the energy of life flows. These are your link, sometimes called the Arc of Light or Rainbow Bridge, to your inner and outer worlds. They are your connection to wholeness and the integration of polarity. Through these you are creating your reality. You have streams of consciousness running up and down and around your body that allow you to receive and transmit. These energy centres are called Chakras and you have many of them throughout your body. Five alone in each hand. You may be more familiar with the seven main ones. They are spinning wheels of electromagnetic energy and if these wheels are out of whack, then your flow is in disharmony. You are not firing on all cylinders and your reception is disrupted.

Your chakras download and receive cosmic universal energy from the unified field to electrify your body, mind and spirit with vitality. These chakras must be in balance for they enhance your lifeforce and allow you to manage and optimize its flow, creating complete cohesion within the physical and its communication with non-physical. We are a flawlessly designed, whole integrated system that works perfectly when in divine accord.

Your lower three chakras are involved in the denser aspects of life in the physical realm, whereas your top three chakras are your connection to the higher part of you. Your Heart chakra is the portal between the two. As we start our ascension journey, we start moving up and living primarily from the upper chakras, but this can only happen when all the lower chakras are in balance.

This is how you consciously create reality in the continuous moment of Now utilizing all your Chakra's when they are in balance.
It starts with the complete integration of the human 'being'. From the connection and understanding of Source energy flowing through all aspects of the human and spirit self to the grounding to Earth. This enables the All to have the sensation and knowing of the complete experience.
1) Through the Crown and awareness of no thing and no one and nothingness, to the vibrating idea for the moment of Now.
2) Then the creation of form through visualization and manipulation of energy to mold the expected physical reality in the Third Eye.
3) To the expression and verbalization with others at the Throat,
4) To the relationship to the environment and others at the Heart.
5) Down through to the Solar Plexus and the perception of it through the tangible senses of touch, taste, smell, sight, and sound. To the expression of delight or displeasure, as an act of will, a perceptual choicepoint.
 6) Allowing the movement through the experience to the emotions, felt and assimilated at the Sacral.
7) To the physical sensation at the Root, followed by the

transmutation to the earth, then back to the Crown. The
encompassing donut of the torus field energy. Where it
starts again.
And again and again in the continuous creation of the
moment of Now, for the fun and feel of it. For evolution
and expansion, what next, what next, what next.

Unconscious creation of reality, will start at the blocked
chakra and travel downwards to earth, meaning often that
alignment is not part of the process. An incomplete
experience cut off from divine direction.

These chakras need to flow in harmony, or it will affect the
functionality of the physical, emotional and mental body.
Overactive, underactive or blocked chakras will lead to dis-
ease, a lack of grounding and off kilter behavior, out of
alignment with your true nature.
Often the flow through the chakras is disturbed from fear,
past experiences and disharmonic belief structures. Blocks
usually occur when you are faced with overwhelming
situations and a rush of charge that you cannot assimilate.
These blocks eventually become obstacles not just from
allowing your energy to free flow, but preventing you from
living full potential lives in mastery and connection.
If the chakra is overactive there is an excess of energy
which can lead to manic behavior, anxiety and
overcompensation.
Underactive, and the system lacks the energy to function,
leading to lethargy, disillusionment, depression and

avoidance behaviours.

Understanding each chakra and which part of the body and which level of consciousness it correlates to will help you to have a better comprehension of yourself. Which areas of your life, either physically or psychologically, you may need to address to bring about balance.

Everyone needs this information, it should be taught to children.

Each chakra has its own frequency and will respond to sound at specific Hertz.

They each correspond to glands within your body and to the energy bands around your body that generate your aura.

They each have their own corresponding colour of the spectrum and when all the colours are put together you are essentially a beam of light. A light being of information and access to information. A receiver and a transmitter. Your root and your crown chakras are like a pillar of light coming from Source energy at your crown through the top of your head all the way through your body and exiting at your root and grounding into the earth. The other chakras radiate out in front of you and at your back.

It has been called the rainbow bridge as it connects your mind to your heart, heaven to earth, spirit to physical. A vertical column of energy that is your route to consciousness.

When they are in balance, you will feel more passion, animation, life. You will experience more synchronicities as your Source finds it easier for you to be receptive to communication.

To begin your transformation, start by walking tall, lift your head, straighten your spine. Allow that light beam of energy to be transmitted through you from Source to Gaia, allow the love to flow through you. A fully integrated, embodied, divine being.

There are many different and varied energy healing practices that will help you reconnect with the energetic part of you. It is very important to note that these methods promote the ability for everyone to find their own healing. In many instances, you will only need one session as the practitioner facilitates your own discovery of how to look after yourself energetically, which will help you physically, emotionally and psychologically. However, Yoga and Qi Gong are continuous practices and lifestyle choices.

I will list and give a brief description of each below. I have used many of them to some degree and have even become a practitioner or attended workshops. They have helped me understand and align with the higher part of myself.

The Western medicine available today focuses on the treatment of the presented symptoms manifested in the physical body only. Or if the problem is psychological, it will try and suppress, through chemicals and other invasive treatments, the perceived dysfunction. This

methodology ignores the fact that we are an energetic embodiment of psychological, emotional and physical aspects, and our treatment should address the whole. Western medicine tries to separate and treat each component, which causes more dis-ease and discomfort and will most likely lead to a lifetime of prescription drug dependency. Such an approach can end up blocking our innate healing abilities without ever addressing the root cause.
Bear in mind that your belief in either, will be the deciding factor between health and dis-ease.

Yoga
Yoga is the Sanskrit word for 'Union'. The practice of Yoga is to unify body, mind and spirit. It is a complete system of movement, meditation, breathing and focus that assists the whole of the individual stay in balance. Yoga, as originally designed, is an eight-fold path (Ashtanga) of wholistic and integrated living. Encapsulating the physical, emotional, spiritual and social parts of existing. It promotes physical health through movement of various postures, called Asanas that build strength and flexibility. Through focus on the breath and the postures it creates a stillness and concentration that benefits the mind. Meditation is an integral part of yoga philosophy, as connection to the divine is paramount to complete living. There are also cleansing routines and an Ayurvedic approach to health that is based on the principle that the

body is the temple of the soul. This promotes balance and harmony, rather than imbalance and then cure. The basic principle is do no harm, to self or others.

It has become popular in western societies as people become more conscious of their health and fitness. This guided fitness session, requires focus and is helping many individuals find moments where the stresses of their lives can, for an hour, be pushed aside. In that moment of stillness, they may just hear something beautiful inside them, whisper something so meaningful, that the doorway to the answers they seek, is nudged ajar. In that sublime moment yoga becomes the gateway for harried Westerners to start their incredible journey back to self.

Qi Gong

Qi Gong or Chi Kung is a system of movement and a very gentle form of exercise. It is a routine of repeated moves that strengthen and stretch the body. This, increases and eases the flow of body fluids, enhancing balance and improving the awareness of how the body moves through space. It also harnesses focused stillness, which allows you to feel the energy in your body and around you. Eventually as you become more attuned to this energy you can manoeuvre and manipulate it. Qi Gong becomes a movement meditation.

Quantum Healing Hypnosis Technique™ – QHHT®
This is a healing modality designed and discovered by Dolores Cannon that guides the client through an induction and relaxation process to bring them to a somnambulistic state of trance. Once here and through visualization and guidance from the practitioner. The higher self, superconscious, or SC of the individual is accessed and can start assisting with the healing process of the individual. The SC is your Higher Self, your broader perspective in the stream of energy consciousness, also called your soul. It has unlimited access to the information of your life and lives, your purpose, and any question that you have. It loves you unconditionally and any information provided to you will be for your highest good and healing. All QHHT® practitioners have been exposed to the high levels of unconditional love and energy this state of consciousness reveals in their training. Their warmth, compassion and kindness while you are in their sessions means that this is a safe, friendly environment to have such a mystical, magical healing experience.

www.blueprint4evolution.com
www.qhhtofficial.com
www.dolorescannon.com

Psychology Kinesiology – Psych-K®
This is a quick, calm and effective process of establishing communication with an individual's sub-conscious mind

and changing self-limiting and self-destructive belief systems and patterns. It was discovered by Robert M. Williams through divine guidance and has been proven to be a simple but powerful tool in healing. Your reality is created by your beliefs and if they are self-sabotaging, you will find that unwanted patterns and experiences keep repeating themselves. Your sub-conscious mind is your hard drive and with the Psych-K® practitioner to guide you, you can rewrite the software by giving it new, positive goal statements to operate from. This method is fantastic and healing because it removes the need to keep talking and focusing on problems and traumatic experiences, and thus reliving them. You simply change the belief or the emotional reaction to an event and you can move on to creating a life free of self-limitation.

www.psych-k.com
www.blueprint4evoluion.com

Chakra Energy Healing
This can be from an energy healer or a reiki practitioner, and can be likened to a healing hands massage. First, the practitioner will open the chakras in their own hands and centre and ground themselves energetically. They will then set a clear intention to allow energy from Source to be channeled through them for the highest good of the client and to create the best healing for them. The practitioner may use a pendulum or specific hand placement to open the chakras and move energy through the body until it is in

alignment and balanced. The client will be fully clothed and the practitioners hands barely or do not touch their body as the energy of each chakra corresponds to the layers in the subtle body or auric field around the body.

Meditation

This is the practice of quieting your mind and finding stillness. This stops the continuous chatter of our unconscious mind, and its distractions. This then allows us to receive communication, feelings of immense love and guidance from the higher perspective part of us. Opening up to our true self. There are many other benefits for meditation. It removes stress, allows relaxation and calmness. It will instantly raise your vibration as you connect to Source energy. It helps with concentration and clarity. Often, we receive inspired thoughts during meditation.

It is the mindfulness of living in the Now, and can be done anywhere, while doing most anything. Walking your dogs, washing up, cleaning your house or sitting on a yoga mat or chair. There are 76 benefits of meditation, check out www.liveanddare.com

There are many guided meditations available on YouTube. Below are some suggestions.

Reality Revolution

Brian Scott

Joe T – Hypnotic Labs

Joe Dispenza

Emotional Freedom Technique (EFT)
This is a system of tapping the body at specific points to relieve stress and anxiety. It works as a kind of acupressure, realigning the energy system and easing pain. It has shown to have better results than other standard (mainstream) treatments for depression. Tapping charts can be found on the internet and tutorials are on YouTube.

Sound Healing
Because our body is composed of energy and this energy has a frequency. Sound healing can reattune the energy of our bodies. Harmonic Resonance occurs when two objects are tuned to the same frequency and vibrate in sympathy with each other. Tibetan bowls, musical instruments, chanting and tuning forks are used. Sound therapy has shown improvements in levels of depression, stress, anxiety, cholesterol, blood pressure, pain and heart disease.
Listen to **Mei-lan Mauritius** on YouTube for incredible sound healing journeys. Listening to binaural, gamma and theta frequency music, will also have a healing or calming effect.

www.halogaia.com sound journeys
www.mei-lanmaurits.com sound healing

Colour or Chromo Therapy

This is a safe and colourful method to ease physical symptoms and heal the mind and body using specific colours. These colours of the spectrum, which are generated by frequencies, relate to certain chakras and can balance vibration and promote healing and harmony. We react differently to each colour, for instance, blue is associated with peace and calm, whereas red is associated with action. It is commonly accepted that colour can affect our moods, feelings and emotions.

Neurodynamic or Holotrophic Breathing

Your breath is the inhalation and exhalation of life itself. It is the life force that sustains you. Very often in stressed or anxious individuals, their breathing rate is so shallow, oxygen is barely able to sustain their life support, and thus improve overall wellbeing. Simple techniques of deep breathing will allow more healing and revitalizing energy and oxygen to flow through the body.

There are specific techniques where the breathing rate is changed deliberately, which will then affect the state of consciousness. This is often a transformational experience revealing your connection to the divine.

www.breathworkonline.com and Michael Stone offer live sessions online. In the sessions you are guided by Michael Stone with compassion, understanding and sincere kindness. The energetic connection you feel with the other participants, strewn across the globe, is so reassuring, supportive and beautiful.

Plant Medicine and Shamanic Ritual

There are a variety of natural plant medicines that have been used for many years in traditional cultures for healing. These include but are not limited to Ayahuasca, San Pedro, Mescaline and Magic Mushrooms.

As with any system of healing, it is important that you find what resonates with you. I have been shown the nature of things and had many a giggle on magic mushrooms, but I have no calling to try any of the others. If you do, make sure you do your research and find a reputable healing centre that will ensure your experience is facilitated ethically and with your highest good in mind.
Ayahuasca is an Amazonian plant that is used in a sacred context by indigenous healers in South America. The Ayahuasca brew contains the powerful psychoactive dimethyletryptamine (DMT) and can induce altered states of consciousness. With a trained and compassionate healer in a controlled and supervised setting. This can help access the subconscious and open communication to release trauma and rebalance energies that are often the cause of emotional distress and physical dis-ease.

The psilocybin found in Magic Mushrooms is converted to psilocin in the body and is believed to influence serotonin levels in the brain. It is also a hallucinogenic drug, a doorway to open your perception. The effects have been

said to increase self-awareness, and often bring a spiritual
experience that leads to a desire for self-discovery and
connection to the mystical and spiritual. Studies are
showing that it is an effective treatment for lowering
anxiety in cancer patients and helping with depression.

Art Therapy

Art Therapy is a widely accepted method that integrates
psychotherapeutic techniques with the creative process to
promote mental health and general wellbeing. Studies
have shown that it reduces stress, anxiety and depression.
It assists in developing the creative process and allowing
the exploration of self-expression to gain personal insights.
Intuitive art can be meditative and can often reveal
emotional states and reactions that are cathartic.

Nature

Never underestimate the healing power of nature. It is
free and probably the most accessible for everyone. You
simply need to go outside and look up! It is also very easy
to combine meditation and nature for instant upliftment.

Any creativity is an expression of the divine.
So sing, dance, play music, play poi. Just play.
Write songs, music, letters, poetry.
Write a journal, write a book, write and recite
affirmations.
Paint, draw, sculpt.

Design, visualize, invent, innovate.
All of this is connection and meditation.

⍰

To initially rebalance your chakras, look to any of the
practitioners of energy healing as listed above for
realignment.
Then take responsibility for the flow of life energy through
your body and allow continued ease as you gracefully flow
through life.

Below is a list of the seven main chakras within your body.
How it will manifest in each, if they are balanced,
overactive, blocked or underactive and what you can do to
heal yourself. There are differing beliefs and approaches to
healing and the modalities available. You will be drawn to
the one that resonates with you.

Root or Muladhara Chakra

Red in colour at a frequency of 432Hz.
Its element is earth.
This first chakra correlates to the adrenal glands, where
the hormones of our survival instincts of fight, flight,
freeze or fold are released in times of stress.
On your physical body it is found at the base of the spine
at the perinium and is your grounding connection to Gaia.
It represents all that is solid in your life and pertains to

your survival on the physical, earthly plane. It is the foundation for your basic survival needs. It relates to your feelings of safety, security, your physicality, and identity. When this chakra is in balance you are grounded in your body and by extension to the world around you. You anchor your energy into the manifest world. You are healthy and have a strong energy foundation that creates vitality and a calm, steadfast attitude. You feel secure, optimistic and that the world is safe and stable around you. You have an unwavering identity of self, of family, your tribe and your place in it. You have a solid trust in your self-reliance and abundance.

Physical symptoms of imbalance include weight issues, as this chakra is directly related to your ability to move energy through your body.
As it is found at your base, there will be problems with legs and lower torso, kidneys, bladder, bowel, immune system, blood transport system, lower back and spine.

If it is overactive it will present as any of the following: Restlessness, aggression, excessive negativity, cynicism, eating disorders, greed, paranoia, excessive feelings of insecurity, constantly feeling stressed, fear of any change, hoarding, arrogance, rigidity, materialism, manic mood swings, too much energy.

If it is underactive or blocked it will present as any of the following:

Depression, delusion, difficulty feeling safe, inconsistent work ethic, a lack of trust, lack of confidence and willpower, laziness, defensiveness, a victim mentality, fear is the motivating factor in decision making and being consumed by a concern for physical safety and risk averse.

To keep your first chakra open and balanced.

Meditate.
Get into Nature, sit on the grass or the sand, run your fingers though it and over it, bury your feet in it. Climb in it, swim in it, barefoot walk in it.
Eat healthy and wholesome foods.
Start some form of physical activity.
Build up a storehouse of skills that satisfy your ideas of what you need to be able to do to survive and be safe.
Start cooking and get your hands in the pots.
Start gardening and get your hands in the earth.
Become self-sufficient around your home, create independence.
Make lists of all the positive aspects around you and what you are grateful for.
Eat potatoes, parsnips, garlic, carrots, and all those lovely root vegetables.
Eat high protein beans, peanut butter and paprika.
Start your journey of introspection to root out the belief systems that no longer serve you. Especially any shortage consciousness beliefs.
Find friends and family and have conversations that move

into trust and optimism not denigration.
Play games.
Rescue a cat or dog from a shelter and give it safety in
your home.

Sacral or Svadhistana Chakra

Orange in colour at a frequency of 480Hz.
Its element is water.
It correlates to your reproductive glands, your testes or
ovaries.
This second chakra is found just below the navel at your
reproduction system.
It is your emotional chakra and your seat of creation. From
this you explore life and your relationship to yourself,
others and your environment. This is where you create the
dynamics of your physical expression in your world. It is
your passions, your talents, your power to realize and
utilize your gifts to express the life you want to live. It is
your emotional intelligence and identity and it is from here
you choose how you respond to the seductive forces and
the five senses of your physical world. This is the start of
innovation, art and creativity. It is also your bonds,
friendships and intimate relationships. Your belief in
abundance within yourself and out. Your authenticity,
honour and ethics.

Physical symptoms of imbalance will affect kidneys,

bladder, large intestines, lower spine, pelvis, appendix, sex organs and reproductive system, hips, lymphatic and circulatory system.

If it is overactive it can present as any of the following: Abusive, controlling, dominant, over indulgent, manic, excessive explosive mood swings, over ambitious, inauthentic, excessively competitive, fear of abandonment, emotional instability, fear of change, promiscuity, loss of financial and creative power.

If it is underactive or blocked it can present as any of the following:
lack of confidence, lack of motivation, no self-expression, no creative or artistic abilities, infertility, frigidity, feeling overwhelmed, no imagination, lack of intimate relationships, resentful, guilty or shameful, shy, distrusting, blameful, addictions.

To keep your second chakra open and balanced.

Dance like nobody is watching and release any shame and guilt.
Keep a journal and pour yourself into it.
Paint, colour, design, garden, write, sing, bake, cook.
Anything to start your creative juices flowing.
Play an instrument or learn to play one.
Learn anything, head to Udemy and sign up.
www.udemy.com

Connect with water. Either drink it, bathe in it, or dive into it. Find a lake, stream or sea.
Eat organic whole foods like nuts, seeds, melons and mangos.
Focus on friendships and create relationships that are fulfilling and inspiring.
Meditate.
Become a teacher, yoga, Qi gong, diving. Find whatever you enjoy and become a master at it.
Volunteer once a week.

Solar Plexus or Manipura Chakra

Yellow in colour at a frequency of 528Hz.
Its element is fire.
This third chakra correlates to the pancreas and is found just above the navel around your stomach and digestive system.
This is the chakra directly related to the amount of energy you can generate and your ability to manage it effectively. It is the fire within, your vitality and the power of intention and clarity you present to the world. It is your accountability for yourself and the responsibility you take for your life, health and relationships. It is your good judgement, your decisiveness, and your ability to set a direction of intention and move towards it. It is your willpower and self-discipline, and once an idea is formulated, to create the momentum to bring it to manifestation. When it is balanced, you are assertive and

set clear boundaries and live in harmonious relationships with others and your world. This is your base of personal power, self-respect, optimism, and trust. It is your belief in yourself, in your inspiration and spontaneous action.

An imbalance will physically affect the digestive system, stomach, small intestine, liver, gall bladder, mid spine, spleen and pancreas.

If overactive it can present as any of the following:
Obsessive compulsive behaviour, a need to control the environment, difficulty focusing, short attention span, manipulative, perfectionist, critical, demanding, stubborn, judgmental, aggressive, domineering.

If it is underactive or blocked it can present as any of the following:
Feelings of helplessness, irresponsibility, lack of direction, purpose, ambition and boundaries, laziness, anxiety, fear, inability to focus, confusion, concern about the opinions of others and a people pleaser.

To keep your third chakra open and balanced:

Let go of the past and its traumas.
Play games that stimulate and sharpen your mind.
Keep an appreciation journal.
Meditate.
Focus on deep mindful breathing.

Exercise, especially mindful movement like yoga or qi
gong.
Build your core and internal muscle strength through
Calisthenics or Pole Dancing.
Listen to music and dance.
Learn Poi, a mind and coordination skill, which is also
really cool to watch.
Watch the sunrise and sunset, look at the stars.
Take a walk and observe the colour in your world.
Eat bananas, pineapples, corn and wear yellow to bring
back cheerfulness.

Heart or Anahata Chakra

Green in colour at a frequency of 594Hz.
Its element is air.
It correlates to the Thymus gland.
The fourth chakra is found at the heart. Surrounded by the
ribs and lungs.
This is the centre of the whole energetic system held
within your body. It is the gateway to the core of your
soul. It is the integration point of what is above as is
below. Your heart chakra is devoted to your relationships,
and most importantly, your understanding and capacity
for self-love. This must be balanced for you to live a
healthy life in accordance with your needs and your desire
for healthy relationships. A balanced heart chakra means
first and foremost that the creed 'do no harm' is

paramount, to self and others. Here lives compassion, balanced boundaries, kindness, empathy, peace, unity, spaciousness, connection, integrity, and respect of all on their path and their direction. All trauma has been transmuted into forgiveness and understanding of its purpose on the journey with no regret. This is also where real intimacy in relationships stems from, as vulnerability is seen as invincibility and an unequivocal authenticity is revealed and reveled in. This allows complete truth to blossom for each soul involved. It is inspiration, hopeful and optimistic, with an intrinsic and unconditional love of life, all experiences, and each encounter.

An imbalance will present itself physically in the heart and the lungs, circulatory and vascular system, breasts, ribs, arms, shoulders and the thymus.

If overactive it will present as any of the following:
Overly empathetic and concerned, a need to 'fix' others, poor boundaries, lack of discernment, indiscriminate love or promiscuity, masochistic tendencies, victim or martyr mentality, misuse of love, overly sacrificing manner, loss of personal identity, codependency, possessiveness, anger, conditional love.

If underactive or blocked it will present as any of the following:
paranoia, fear of rejection, indecisiveness, cynicism, meanness, hatred, fear, insecurity, jealousy, grief,

manipulation, disconnection, resentment, bitterness, withdrawn and shy, loner mentality, lack of trust in self and others, no empathy or forgiveness.

To keep your fourth chakra open and balanced:

Face and let go of past traumas and perceived slights.
Accept the responsibility of your own healing.
Keep an honesty and gratitude journal.
Get into nature, let her love you back to your true self.
Get some houseplants and talk to them.
Volunteer at an animal shelter and tell no one.
Get a session with a QHHT® practitioner and speak to your higher self.
Have a massage.
Sound therapy. Listen to Solfeggio frequencies and Mei-lan Mauritius on YouTube.
Attend a Neurodynamic breathwork workshop.
Try an EFT (Emotional Freedom Technique) session.
Yoga.
Meditation.
Eat healthy leafy greens, avocados, apples and cucumbers and broccoli.
Wear green clothes.

Throat or Vishuddha Chakra

Blue in colour at a frequency of 672Hz.

Its element is ether.
It correlates to the thyroid and parathyroid glands.
The fifth chakra is located in the throat.
This is where all communication comes from with yourself and others. Your ability to communicate clearly, concisely and with integrity and authenticity. It is your self-expression and your outer influence. It is also the conduit through which the heart and mind communicate. Any imbalance and it becomes a bottleneck with the potential to explode. It is a pressure valve that allows energy from the other chakras to be expressed. It is where you verbalize the reality you desire and believe in. Your articulation of truth and the honour code you choose to live by. It is also your ability to be a good listener and absorb and assimilate the communications going on around you. Speaking the truth of your beliefs, ideas and emotions will allow you to live in alignment with no hidden agendas. An honest existence of expressed freedom.

An imbalance will present itself physically in the throat and surrounding areas causing problems in the thyroid and parathyroid glands. Jaw and mouth issues. Ears and sinus problems. Weight issues and eating disorders, pain in the back of the head and neck.

If overactive it can present as any of the following:
Habitual or compulsive lying, manipulation, fear and doubt in the words of others, incessant talking, gossiping, degrading self-talk and talk of others. Inability to listen,

interrupting, arrogant and sanctimonious. Dogmatic and critical. Explosive reactions.

If underactive it can present as any of the following: Unreliable, loss of words, timid, shy, small quiet voice, scared, extreme difficulty in expressing feelings, unspoken resentment, and blame. Defensive reactions. Feeling vulnerable and 'trying to handle it all alone'

To keep your fifth chakra open and balanced:

First heal your heart. To express your true self without fear of prejudice, you must first love yourself and trust all that you believe in.
Your boundaries must be clear to you and spoken to others with kindness and clarity.
You must also get to a place where you understand that the opinions of others have no place in your concept of yourself.
You must express all that you have unconsciously held back, so start an unfiltered and private journal.
Write letters to those that you need to express your truth to, even if you don't send them.
Talk to a trusted friend.
Talk to a therapist, but only to express and expunge what is held within, not for continued talking about the problem as this just strengthens its hold.
Have a Pysch-K® and/or QHHT® session
Understand that you have the right to your own voice.

Speak out loud. To yourself, your dogs, the trees.
Develop a supportive inner dialogue.
Work on not reacting in situations, assimilate what is being
said or done and then respond in a kind, clear and
thoughtful manner.
Sing.
Meditate.
Repeat Affirmations similar to 'I express myself honestly,
calmly and with clarity'
Yoga and energy movement.
Sound healing and blue crystals.
Drink coconut water and herbal teas.
Eat fruits that fall from trees, licorice and blue and
blackberries.
Wear blue clothes and accessories.

The Third Eye or Ajna Chakra

Indigo in colour at a frequency of 720Hz.
Its element is light.
It correlates to your pituitary gland.
The sixth chakra is located on your forehead between your
eyebrows.
This chakra is where spiritual awareness starts. It is your
connection to your innate wisdom and your ability to
accept communication from your higher self in the form of
impulse, intuition and inspired action. When blocks are

cleared in the lower chakras and energy flows upward, it creates a link to your higher consciousness, and you are more aware of insight, imagination and visual guidance. You can harness the charge to illuminate your inner world and higher realms. Activation in this chakra allows you to see beyond the illusion of the third density reality. Releasing thought patterns and limiting belief structures and understanding the boundless gifts you have a divine right to. You can change your perception, and thus your experience of reality, with the recognition of non-duality. You have opened your mind to the freedom, inner knowledge and inner sight, gifts us with. You have discernment and are open to new ideas and expansion that resonates within you. You may be able to astral travel and have telepathic abilities. You can see, feel or intuit energy, and be able to manipulate it, as is your birthright.

Imbalance here will manifest physically as seizures, disorders in the endocrine system, strokes, migraines, brain tumours, defects in vision, deafness, sleep disorders and hormonal imbalances.

If it is overactive it can present as any of the following: Religiously dogmatic. A propensity for cognitive dissonance, (where your perceived truth is the only one that can exist, as you are unwilling and unable to look at any idea or evidence that may prove your belief incorrect.) A fierce holding onto of external belief structures that allow for a lack of accountability. No ability or desire for

self-reflection. Denial, (as it would lead to a reevaluation of all life decisions prior to assimilating a new idea. This is unacceptable as it means a change in perception of self. In this instance ignorance is the preferred choice.)
Attachment to identity and roles.
Obsessive, and egomaniacal behaviour, difficulty concentrating, delusions and hallucinations.

If blocked or underactive it can present as any of the following:
Depression, timidity, oversensitivity to the opinions of others, defensive and negative thinking. Anger and resentment. A fear of application of individual thought and a staunch unwillingness to self-reflect or look within. A deep shame and denial of the shadow side or dark nature leading to distortion of self and identity. Afraid of failure and success, undisciplined and unable to visualize. Continuously distracted, unable to remember dreams, lacking imagination.

To keep your sixth chakra open and balanced.

Meditate, there are many guided meditations to open the third eye.
Practice lucid dreaming.
Practice astral travel through guided meditations.
Start your journey to inner knowing, your shadow work and intimate knowledge of self. This will include finding all your limiting beliefs, thoughtforms and patterning.

Have a Psych-k® session to replace destructive belief systems with new goal statements.
Connect with your higher self through QHHT® or self-hypnosis meditations.
Cultivate silence.
Hone your intuition and your immediate acquiescence to its guidance.
Ground yourself in Nature, submerge yourself in it.
Get some moonlight and some sunlight.
Nurture your creative side.
Try Holotrophic or Neurodynamic breathing.
Plant medicine (only if it resonates with you) shamanic ritual and sound.
Eat purple foods like eggplant, prunes, beetroot and blackcurrants.
Where purple clothes and surround yourself with purple.

The Crown or Sahasrara Chakra

Violet in colour and at a frequency of 768Hz.
Its element is cosmic energy.
It correlates to your pineal gland.
This seventh chakra is located on the crown of your head.
This is your gateway to Source energy, the bridge between physical and non-physical, humanity and spirituality.
When the crown chakra is open and balanced this is where you can integrate your connection to Source energy and fully comprehend the limitlessness of all that you are and

allow it to guide your life from a far broader and all-encompassing perspective. It is acknowledgment of the oneness and living in the receivership of transmitted energy that allows the conscious creation of your reality in this moment of Now. Pure conscious awareness will free flow through you in a stream of intelligent, infinite potential energy. Cosmically infused with light and love allowing you to create your dream reality through manifestation and manipulation of the field of information. This is enlightenment, this is being a conscious creator. When open, you, the creator in human form, will be playful, centred, grateful, enthusiastic, cheeky, unconditionally loving, funny and with a full comprehension of yourself as an eternal being, interconnected with everything. You will know that everything and everyone else is also eternal and on their own path. You will have an aura of inner peace, innate mindfulness and non-attachment to outcome as you exist fully in the moment of Now. You will have access to all possible gifts, such as telepathy, clairsentience, clairvoyance, clairaudience, and many more and probably many that are beyond our ability to imagine yet.

An imbalance will manifest in psychological disorders, extreme sensitivity to sound and light and other environmental stimuli. Brain injuries, malfunction and disease. Extreme exhaustion and sleep disorders. Loss of balance, headaches and clumsiness.

If it is overactive it may present as any of the following:
Frustration, elitism, boredom, spiritual arrogance and a
difficulty in staying grounded. A god complex, focused on
the little details and cannot or will not see the bigger
picture.

If it is blocked or underactive it may present as any of the
following:
Depression, mental fog, uninspired, materialistic, lethargic,
a sense of alienation and disconnection. A fear of dying

Blockages are generally caused by stressful lifestyles,
unresolved trauma, conditioned beliefs of separation and
isolation. An identity defined by ego, labels, and others. A
belief that life is happening to you.

To keep your seventh Chakra open and balanced:

Slow down and calm down.
Stop believing all your thoughts.
Accept that there is something utterly miraculous going on
and you can choose to be a part of it (or not) in this
lifetime.
Set clear intentions.
Resolve the issues of your past, through QHHT® and/or
Psych-K®
Educate yourself on the bigger picture and commit to your
own self-discovery.
Keep a journal.

Meditate.
Qi Gong.
Yin Yoga.
Get into nature and allow her stillness to reconnect you to yourself and Source.
Sound healing.
Colour and Art therapy.
Breathwork.

Suggested Research Material

Remember you are a continuously evolving masterpiece.

Stop watching Netflix for a little bit and try Gaia or Magellan Television.

Documentaries or Movies to watch
Superhuman: The Invisible Made Visible
Rewired – Dr. Joe Dispenza
Initiation – Matias De Stefano
The Connected Universe – Nassim Haramein
The Shift – Wayne Dyer
What the Bleep Do We Know
The Living Universe
Enlightenment
PHI movie

Samsara

Finding Joe

Aluna

Samadhi

The Art of Living Effortlessly

The Earthing Movie

Waking Life

I Origins

Conversations With God

The Secrets of Quantum Physics

The Celestine Prophecy

Kymatica

I AM

Inner Worlds, Outer Worlds

Fierce Grace – Ram Dass

The Five People You Meet In Heaven

Awake, The Life Of Yogananda

Paradise or Oblivion – The Venus Project

The Nature of Ayahuasca

Websites to explore, online courses, science and consciousness information

www.drjoedispenza.com
www.abraham-hicks.com
www.gaia.com
www.superhumanfilm.com

www.resonancescience.org

www.blueprint4evolution.com

www.halogaia.com

www.heartmath.com

www.wimhofmethod.com

www.sarahblondin.com

www.tarabrach.com

www.chakraschool.thinkific.com

www.scienceandnonduality.com

www.qhhtofficial.com

www.psych-k.com

www.breathworkonline.com

www.theshiftnetwork.com

www.mindvalley.com

www.spiritpathways.co.za

www.anodeajudith.com

www.themindbodyspiritnetwork.com

www.yogalap.com

www.radicalhappiness.com

www.awakeningself.com

www.transformingourselves.com

www.thevenusproject.com

www.reiki.org

www.harmonicsound.com

www.holisticlighttherapy.com

www.jamyeprice.com

www.colourtherapyhealing.com

Suggested Books to read
Science, Psychology, Hypnotherapy

Dr. Joe Dispenza author of
Breaking the Habit of Being Yourself
Becoming Supernatural
Evolve Your Brain
You Are the Placebo

Dr. Bruce Lipton author of
The Biology of Belief
Spontaneous Evolution
The Honeymoon Effect

Masaru Emoto author of
The Hidden Messages in Water

Wim Hof author of
The Wim Hof Method
Becoming The Iceman
Way of The Iceman
The Iceman Speaks

Dr. Wayne Dyer author of
Your Erroneous Zones
The Power Of Intention
Change Your Thoughts, Change Your Life
Wishes Fulfilled

I Can Clearly See Now
There's a Spiritual Solution to Every Problem
Manifest Your Destiny
Excuses Begone!

Dr. Tara Brach author of
Finding True Refuge
Radical Acceptance
Radical Compassion
A Year Of Living With More Compassion

Dr. Brian Weiss author of
Many Lives Many Masters
Only Love Is Real
Through Time To Healing
Same Soul Many Bodies

Dr. Lynne McTaggart author of
The Intention Experiment
The Field
The Power Of Eight
The Bond

Dolores Cannon author of
The Three Waves Of Volunteers and The New Earth
Jesus and The Essenes
Keepers Of The Garden
The Convoluted Universe 1,2 and 3

Between Death and Life
Conversations With Nostradamus
Five Lives Remembered

Robert M. Williams author of
Psych-K®: The Missing Peace In Your Life

Gregg Braden author of
The Divine Matrix
The God Code
The Isaiah Effect
The Spontaneous Healing of Belief
Secrets of The Lost Mode Of Prayer
Fractal Time
The Science of Self-Empowerment
The Wisdom Codes
Deep Truth
Resilience From The Heart
Human By Design
Walking Between The Worlds
Spiritual Teachings

Abraham Hicks/Esther Hicks author of
The Law Of Attraction
Ask and It Is Given
The Vortex
Money and The Law Of Attraction
The Astonishing Power of Emotions

The Amazing Power of Deliberate Intent
Getting Into The Vortex
Manifest Your Desires

Eckhart Tolle author of
The Power Of Now
A New Earth
Stillness Speaks
Guardians Of Being
Oneness With All Life

Anodea Judith author of
Wheels Of Life
The Chakra System
Creating On Purpose
The Global Heart Awakens
Charge and The Energy Body

Other Suggested Books

Reality Transurfing - Vadim Zeland
The Alchemist – Paulo Coelho
The Prophet - Kahlil Gibran
Conversations With God 1-3 – Neal Donald Walsh
The Celestine Prophecy – James Redfield
What Is Lightbody? Archangel Ariel – Tashira Tachi-ren
The Art of Happiness – Dalai Lama
The Essential Rumi - Rumi
The Four Agreements - Don Miguel Ruiz

Women Who Run With Wolves – Clarissa Pinkola Estes

The Zen Teachings of Bodhidharma

The Seven Treasuries - Longchenpa

The Law Of One Ra Material – Carla Rueckert, Don Elkins, James Allen McCarty

The Ultimate Happiness Prescription – Deepak Chopra

The Gifts Of Imperfection – Brene Brown

Think and Grow Rich – Napoleon Hill

Biocentrism – Robert Lanza

Good Vibes Good Life – Vex King

The Subtle Art of Not Giving a F*ck- Mark Manson

Atomic Habits – James Clear

Get Out of Your Head – Jennie Allen

The following are YouTube channels

Abraham Hicks

Dr. Joe Dispenza

Gregg Braden

Bruce Lipton

Blueprint For Evolution

Rob Williams Psych – K®

Alan Watts

Awakening You AA Michael

Esther Rouah

Sarah Blondin

Teal Swan
Aaron Doherty
Aluna Ash
Russell Brand
Eckhart Tolle
Dr. Wayne Dyer
Mark Houghten and Deliberate Creators
Aaron Abke
Brian Scott and the Reality Revolution
Neville Goddard
Bashar

Though I have tried to focus on how to raise your vibration
and to dig deep to understand who you are. That to
change the world, you change yourself.
I feel it would be remiss of me not to include some of the
documentaries and books that provide information on the
structures that you have allowed to distract, divide and
control you.
You may feel that you need to watch these if they
resonate with you and you need the information to break
through any cognitive dissonance you have.
However going down these roads can lead to anger,
distrust, despair and this will lower your vibration.
Ultimately what you resist, persists. Any belief system is
sustained by your energetic focus upon it, whether
positive or negative.
Remember also that your ego self is always looking for

someone or something external to blame. These
documentaries provide that, allowing you to believe your
world was perpetrated to you.
If you understand the concepts in this book, then just
apply them.
As fighting against something, is like shouting for quiet. It
is ineffective and just creates more of what you don't want
as per The Law of Attraction.

Zeitgeist
A Virus Called Fear
The Oil Factor
The World According to Montsanto

Cosmic Joke

All That Is: Its nice here in the void of All That Is, isn't it..?
Me (Also All That Is): Yes it is, but I would really like to experience what All That Is, is.
All That Is: Ok you can do that, but to experience All That Is you must experience All That Is Not, and that can only be done in a physical, three dimensional construct of separation.
Me (Also All That Is): Ok, let's do it.
All That Is: Ok cool, it's done. And I made Coffee!
Me (Also All That Is): Ok cool, see you later.
All That Is: Hahaha no, no.. see you NOW....!!!

Author's Note

Two best friends. Three stray dogs.
An eco-lodge built from scratch in the middle of nowhere, the cyclone that blew it down, and the team that rebuilt it can provide a lot of life lessons. But that is another story. This book is inspired by the white doggy. She eventually went blind, but still runs down the beach, nose in the air and tail wagging. A walking (or running) philosophy of life.

This book has been written with the sole intention of asking the reader to consider the wondrous magic of life, and to be curious of their relationship and purpose within its magnificent expression. The tenets shared in this book can inspire questions, maybe a request for clarity and hopefully some discussion and discourse.
I ask you to please contact me.
I am excitedly, hoping that we can start a connection and a chat about anything that creates momentum towards our understanding and expansion. I promise that I will read and answer all emails personally and any constructive

criticism is always welcome. I hope that this book will activate the inevitable journey to higher consciousness for as many of us as possible.

So, I ask you dear reader, to please give a moment of your time and post a review of this book on Amazon.

Amazon.com link:

https://www.amazon.com/review/create-review/error?&asin=B08GYWM8Y2

Amazon.co.uk link:

https://www.amazon.co.uk/review/create-review/error?&asin=B08GYWM8Y2

I ask this with deep gratitude, so as to enhance its capability to reach the hands and open hearts of others seeking a handbook such as this.

I know we are one and I love you.

I love you so much.

Liz Nottage

Email: alignupmindfully@gmail.com

FaceBook: Liz Nottage

FaceBook page: Align Up Mindfully